Studies in Economic History

Series Editor

Tetsuji Okazaki, Faculty of Economics, The University of Tokyo, Tokyo, Japan

Aims and Scope

This series from Springer provides a platform for works in economic history that truly integrate economics and history. Books on a wide range of related topics are welcomed and encouraged, including those in macro-economic history, financial history, labor history, industrial history, agricultural history, the history of institutions and organizations, spatial economic history, law and economic history, political economic history, historical demography, and environmental history.

Economic history studies have greatly developed over the past several decades through application of economics and econometrics. Particularly in recent years, a variety of new economic theories and sophisticated econometric techniques—including game theory, spatial economics, and generalized method of moment (GMM)—have been introduced for the great benefit of economic historians and the research community.

At the same time, a good economic history study should contribute more than just an application of economics and econometrics to past data. It raises novel research questions, proposes a new view of history, and/or provides rich documentation. This series is intended to integrate data analysis, close examination of archival works, and application of theoretical frameworks to offer new insights and even provide opportunities to rethink theories.

The purview of this new Springer series is truly global, encompassing all nations and areas of the world as well as all eras from ancient times to the present. The editorial board, who are internationally renowned leaders among economic historians, carefully evaluate and judge each manuscript, referring to reports from expert reviewers. The series publishes contributions by university professors and others well established in the academic community, as well as work deemed to be of equivalent merit.

All books and chapters in the Studies in Economic History book series are indexed in Scopus.

More information about this series at http://www.springer.com/series/13279

Masato Shizume

The Japanese Economy During the Great Depression

The Emergence of Macroeconomic Policy in A Small and Open Economy, 1931–1936

Springer

Masato Shizume
Faculty of Political Science and Economics
Waseda University
Tokyo, Japan

ISSN 2364-1797 ISSN 2364-1800 (electronic)
Studies in Economic History
ISBN 978-981-13-7356-5 ISBN 978-981-13-7357-2 (eBook)
https://doi.org/10.1007/978-981-13-7357-2

This Springer imprint is published by the registered company Springer Nature Singapore Pte Ltd.
The registered company address is: 152 Beach Road, #21-01/04 Gateway East, Singapore 189721, Singapore

Takahashi Korekiyo in his garden, 1930, by courtesy of Yasushi Inoue

Preface

This book project began sometime around 2000, when I was working for the Institute for Monetary and Economic Studies (IMES), Bank of Japan (BOJ). One day, I had a conversation with Masaaki Shirakawa, then head of the Policy Planning Office and later governor of the BOJ (2008–2013), about the lessons to be learned from Takahashi Korekiyo's policies. Mr. Shirakawa asked me what lessons the central bank today could derive from Takahashi's experience during the Great Depression. I replied that to answer that question, we would need further research on the challenges Takahashi faced, Takahashi's intentions, and the similarities and differences between Takahashi's time and today.

Two decades have since passed. During this time, I have published several papers in English and Japanese, written a book on Takahashi's policies in the 1930s in Japanese (Shizume 2009), and translated Takahashi's biography, originally written in English (Smethurst 2007), into Japanese. These tasks gave me the opportunity to dig into new archival materials, construct new data sets for econometric analyses, obtain new insights, and raise new questions. I also, in 2014, left the BOJ to take up a position at Waseda University. The new environment provided me a fresh perspective for my research.

When I finished my book in Japanese in 2009, I thought it might be a good idea to rewrite it in English. I also thought I would share the data set I had constructed and add more econometric analysis to further explore the nature of Takahashi's policies to introduce his achievements to a broader audience. Thanks to the cooperation of Springer Nature, I have completed my thesis in English. The full data set used in this volume is available on the website of the Research Institute for Economics and Business Administration (RIEB), Kobe University.[1]

With the passage of time, the BOJ has continued to enhance its unconventional monetary policy. In the wake of the global financial crisis of 2008, other central banks in mature economies followed suit. The change in the tide of global economics, geopolitics, and domestic politics in a number of countries sheds new light on the

[1] The data are available on the Kobe University RIEB website: http://ccss.kobe-u.ac.jp/en/research/database/.

historical lessons to be learned from macroeconomic policy as well as from international relations. COVID-19 has brought new challenges for policymakers around the world in both economic and political spheres. It has also completely changed academic life. For some time starting the spring of 2020, virtually all classes in universities were held online, and conferences and seminars were either cancelled or postponed. Interactions with students and colleagues continue to be restricted, making us freshly aware of the importance of face-to-face communications. Conferences and seminars are now regularly being held online, thanks to information technology. Universities in Japan are preparing to resume classroom teaching while continuing with online and hybrid styles of teaching. I have come to feel in a broad sense that crises bring innovations, a key phrase I use in connection with Takahashi's policy innovations.

Since the start of this project, I have extended the scope of my research, and the book's perspective ended up broader than I had originally intended. I have added an analysis on the political economy of Takahashi's policy formation with reference to modern Japan's national goal from long-term and global perspectives. The 1930s tested the "rich country, strong military" goal of Meiji Japan as an emerging nation state. There were multiple challenges arising from the international–domestic and economic–political nexuses. I have come to be convinced that the challenges Takahashi faced, the sources of his ideas, and the consequences of the choices made by the Japanese government and people hold precious lessons for us, in the twenty-first century, in a world with challenges comparable to Takahashi's own. The research is still ongoing, and I will continue to do my part, but I hope this book raises new questions and brings opportunities for new projects.

I thank all who have encouraged and helped me complete this volume. Richard Smethurst and Mark Metzler, two distinguished historians and experts in modern Japanese economy and society, have provided advice, suggestions, and invaluable insights throughout. Masahiko Shibamoto provided econometric support, gave suggestions on data and methodology, and permitted me to publish the data we constructed in our joint research. Yasuo Takatsuki and staff of Center for Computational Social Science (CCSS), RIEB, Kobe University, also supported my publication of this data. Mark Metzler has read the whole book, Patrice Baubeau and Junko Koeda have read a chapter, and all of them have given me valuable feedback. All remaining errors are of my own. I benefitted greatly from the archival materials of the Bank of Japan Archives, the Bank of England Archives, the National Archives of Japan, the National Diet Library of Japan, and the Kobe University and Waseda University libraries. This work was supported by JSPS KAKENHI Grant Number 18H00660. Last but not least, I would like to thank Tetsuji Okazaki, series editor of the Studies in Economic History book series and the editorial board members of the book series as well as Juno Kawakami, the editor at Springer, who has dedicated herself to ensure the publication of this book.

Tokyo, Japan
March 2021

Masato Shizume

References

Shizume, Masato. 2009. *Sekai kyōkō to keizai seisaku: kaihō shōkoku Nihon no keiken to gendai* (The world depression and economic policy: lessons from Japan as a small open economy). Tokyo: Nikkei Shinbun Shuppan Sha.

Smethurst, Richard J. 2007. *From foot soldier to finance minister: Takahashi Korekiyo, Japan's Keynes*. Cambridge, MA: Harvard University Asia Center, 292.

Contents

About the Author

Masato Shizume is Professor of economics at Waseda University. His research focuses on the history of money and credit and the emergence and developments of the modern society and state in Japan. He has published articles, books, and chapters on the monetary history of Japan in both English and Japanese. His recent publications include *The Emergence and Developments of Credit Money: Evidence from the Pre-modern Period to the Present*, 2020 (editor, in Japanese); "Strategic Central Bank Communication: Discourse Analysis of the Bank of Japan's Monthly Report", *Journal of Economic Dynamics and Control*, vol. 100, 2019 (with Kohei Kawamura, Yōhei Kobashi, and Kōzō Ueda); "Historical Evolution of Monetary Policy (Goals and Instruments) in Japan: From the Central Bank of an Emerging Economy to the Central Bank of a Mature Economy", Stefano Battilossi, Youssef Cassis, and Kazuhiko Yago, editors, *Handbook of the History of Money and Currency*, 2018; "A History of the Bank of Japan, 1882–2016", Tor Jacobson, Daniel Waldenström, and Rodney Edvinsson, editors, *Sveriges Riksbank 350 Years: A Central Bank in a World of Central Banks*, 2018; and "Financial Crises and the Central Bank: Lessons from Japan during the 1920s", Hugh Rockoff and Isao Suto, editors, *Coping with Financial Crises: Some Lessons from Financial History*, 2018. His undergraduate degree is from Keio University, and his Ph.D. is from Kobe University.

Abbreviations

BIS	Bank for International Settlements
BOJ	Bank of Japan
FRB	Federal Reserve Board
GBP	British pound sterling
GHQ/SCAP	General Headquarters of the Supreme Commander for the Allied Powers
GNP	Gross national product
IMES	Institute for Monetary and Economic Studies
JGBs	Japanese government bonds
JPY	Japanese yen
LOLR	Lender of last resort
LTES	Long-Term Economic Statistics (Hitotsubashi University)
MOF	Ministry of Finance
ODR	Official discount rate
PCA	Principal component analysis
RIEB	Research Institute for Economics and Business Administration
S-VAR	Structural vector autoregression
TSE	Tokyo Stock Exchange
USD	US dollar
WPI	Wholesale price index
ZLB	Zero lower bound

List of Figures

List of Tables

Chapter 1
Takahashi Korekiyo, the Man Who Brought Japan Out of the Great Depression

In this book, I revisit the achievements of Takahashi Korekiyo, a finance minister of Japan whose innovative macroeconomic policy brought Japan out of the global Great Depression in the 1930s. To this end, I review the Japanese economy in this period with data and chronology, explore the origins, intentions, and the consequences of Takahashi's policy with econometric and archival analyses, and discuss lessons from this policy that can be applied today. In this introductory chapter, I go through the Japanese economy with reference to Takahashi's policy and show the goals and the structure of this book.

1.1 Japan's Great Depression Hero

Takahashi Korekiyo (1854–1936), a Japanese statesman with an impressive track record as finance minister, lived through the period of modernization and globalization in the late nineteenth and early twentieth centuries. He was born in Edo (now Tokyo) in 1854, the year in which the Tokugawa shogunate concluded the Treaty of Peace and Amity between the United States and Japan. He acquired a high level of English-language proficiency, first in Yokohama, the newly opened treaty port town, and then in the United States. He went on to work in several private- and public-sector positions, including in the Agriculture and Commerce Ministry of the new Meiji Government, where he helped draft proposals for the promotion of industry (*Kōgyō Iken*; Opinions on the Promotion of Industry). He joined the Bank of Japan (BOJ) in 1892, represented the Japanese government in overseas fundraising activities during the Russo-Japanese War (1904–1905), and served as governor of the BOJ from 1911 to 1913.

Starting his first appointment as finance minister in 1913, Takahashi served as finance minister five times in seven administrations until his assassination in 1936. When he returned to office in December 1931, he was already widely recognized for

M. Shizume, *The Japanese Economy During the Great Depression*, Studies in Economic History,
https://doi.org/10.1007/978-981-13-7357-2_1

his capabilities in public finance, backed by a wealth of experience and a prominent presence in the domestic policymaking arena as well as in the international financial markets. The Japanese economy had plunged into double-digit deflation and negative real economic growth as a result of the global depression and the lifting of the gold embargo in January 1930 implemented under the initiative of Finance Minister Inoue Junnosuke, Takahashi's predecessor.

While the Great Depression was a global event (Temin 1989; Eichengreen 1992; James 2001), Japan was unique in the sense that it was doubly hit because of its return to the gold standard at the worst timing of January 1930, just before the depression deepened and spread all over the world (Patrick 1971: 252–256).

Takahashi has been often referred to as one of the world's best policy innovators during the Great Depression of the 1930s. He implemented a quintessentially Keynesian macroeconomic stimulus package (*Takahashi zaisei*, or the Takahashi fiscal package) combining a massive currency depreciation, fiscal stimulus, and monetary easing, to lift the Japanese economy (Nakamura 1983; Nakamura and Odaka 1999; Shibamoto and Shizume 2014). Among other policy innovations, Takahashi and his colleagues, or "Team Takahashi," designed a new scheme of open market operations and the underwriting of government bonds by the central bank.

Takahashi's policy package predated Keynes' *General Theory*, which was published in 1936. Later economists and economic historians have dubbed Takahashi "the Keynesian before Keynes" (Flath 2005; Smethurst 2007). Thanks to Takahashi's policies, Japan emerged from its deflationary spiral and made a robust economic recovery well ahead of other major countries. Japan's real GDP growth and price recoveries outpaced those of other major countries (Figs. 1.1, 1.2).

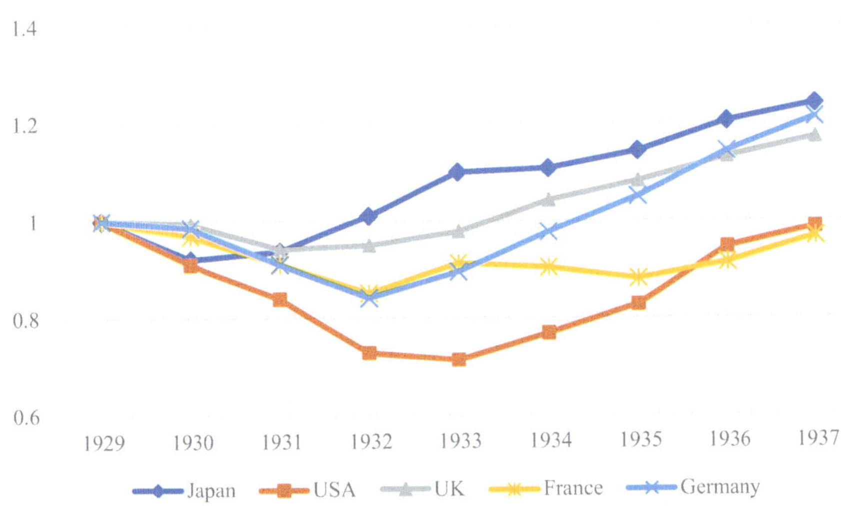

Fig. 1.1 GDP in selected countries (1929 = 1). *Source* Historical Statistics of the World Economy, the Maddison Project; Fukao et al. (2017)

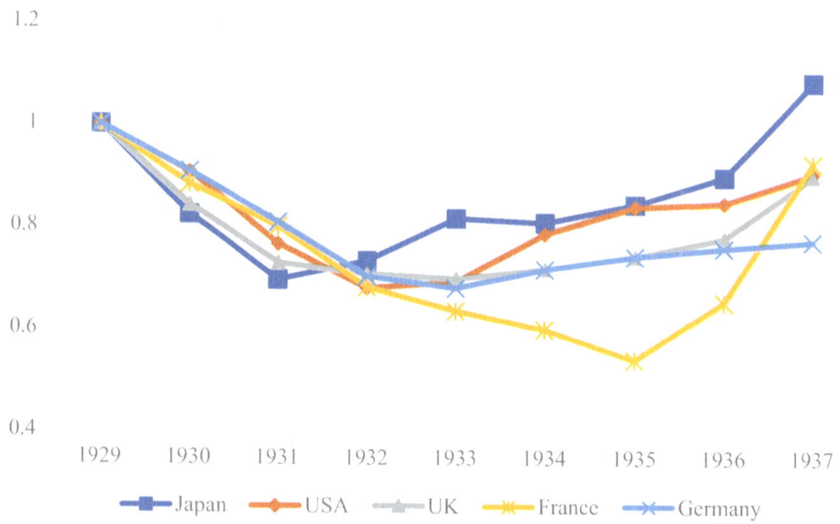

Fig. 1.2 CPI of selected countries (1929 = 1). *Source Statistical Yearbook of the League of Nations*, various issues

In 2003, then board member of the Federal Reserve Board (FRB) Ben Bernanke, who would later (2006–2014) serve as the FRB chairman, praised Takahashi in a speech before Japanese monetary economists, saying "Takahashi brilliantly rescued Japan from the Great Depression through reflationary policies in the early 1930s" (Bernanke 2003).

Takahashi's era has been perceived in one of two ways, either as an era of economic militarization with social dumping and inflation, or for his success in his Keynesian experiment (Nakamura 1983: 232). Recent studies in Japanese history have explored the crises under a newly emerged two-party parliamentary system in Japan from three perspectives: the crisis in the economic sphere, the crisis in international relations, and the crisis in domestic politics (Inoue 2012: 241). As such, the era was full of challenges and opportunities. The decision-making process under the Meiji Constitution and its transformation over time put constraints on Takahashi's policy choices, which forbids a simplistic interpretation based on superficial observations. We need to consider the political economy and underlying social transformation of interwar Japan. I will explore the topic while referring to a preliminary analysis in Shizume (2009, 2011) and updated literature in the political history of interwar Japan.

Which part of Takahashi's policy package was effective still remains debatable. Nanto and Takagi (1985: 374) claim that "the importance of price factors—primarily brought about by Takahashi's exchange rate policies—in the subsequent economic recovery is clearly indicated. On the other hand, the contribution of fiscal policies…may well have been given too much credit." Kindleberger (1973: 242) also states that "much of the impetus for the expansion came from the international margin as a result of the undervaluation of the yen." Meanwhile, Eichengreen (1992: 309) notes that "the imperative of financing military spending provided the main impetus for expansion."

Nanto and Takagi (1985) forego interpreting the effect and the transmission mechanism of Takahashi's policy package due to data constraints, stating that the "[U]se of monthly or even quarterly data might provide a better basis for interpreting the causal relationships observed among different economic variables, if such time-series were available." In this regard, we have recently seen substantial progress. Cha (2003: 136) employs a structural vector-auto-regression (S-VAR) analysis using monthly data and concludes that "Takahashi's deficit spending was indeed crucial in ending the depression quickly." Shibamoto and Shizume (2014) refines Cha's method of S-VAR by adding a variable representing the expectation channel and concludes that "the exchange rate adjustment undertaken as an independent policy tool had the strongest effect," showing that Cha's analysis suffers from a problem of missing variables. In this book, I will elaborate on this topic with reference to Shibamoto and Shizume (2014).

When Takahashi returned to office at the end of 1931, the international environment was deteriorating. The Great Depression was intensifying and spreading globally. Attempts to restore the international monetary regime were on the verge of collapse following the British departure from the gold standard. Tensions with a big neighbor, China, were in a heightened state due to Japanese aggression in mainland China. On the domestic front, the Japanese economy took a double hit from the ill-fated return to the gold standard and the Great Depression.

A two-party parliamentary democracy had emerged during the 1910s and 1920s. The Rikken-Seiyūkai (hereafter Seiyūkai) party was established in 1900, based on the interests of rural landowners with conservative traditions. The Kenseikai party was established in 1916 based on the interests of urban businesses with liberal, progressive assertions. The Kenseikai was reorganized into the Rikken-Minseitō (hereafter Minseitō) party in 1927. The two-party system proceeded along with the constitutional implementation of universal male suffrage in 1925 (Inoue 2012). Yet, the early 1930s has been perceived as a period of transition from one with liberal economic policies and a parliamentary democracy toward wartime command economy and fascism (Gordon 1991; Metzler 2006). After the Mukden Incident in September 1931, three months before Takahashi's return to office, the Japanese army in Manchuria initiated undeclared war with China and committed to it through his term.

On February 26, 1936, Takahashi's term as finance minister was cut short when a group of militarists assassinated him and his colleagues following his refusal to increase the military budget. Takahashi had refused because he was convinced that the Japanese economy had reached full employment and that the time had come to refrain from a further increase in fiscal spending. "So, Takahashi's economic policy ended with a catastrophe" (Bank of Japan 1984: 170). The year after that, Japan headed into the Second Sino-Japanese War, which led the country into the Asia–Pacific War, and then on to lose its sovereignty for the first time in its entire history. Some historians claim that fiscal stimulus with debt financing under Takahashi's leadership paved the way for a loss of fiscal discipline (Shima 1983: 117–120, Metzler 2006: 243–244).

Some observers claim that Takahashi may have been inspired by Keynes' work predating his *General Theory*. Nanto and Takagi (1985: 372) point to an influential pamphlet Keynes coauthored with Hubert Henderson in 1929 entitled "Can Lloyd George Do It?" and suggests that "it is quite likely that (Takahashi) had read the Keynesian description of the expenditure multiplier by 1929," whereas Smethurst (2007: 305–306) concludes that "it is unclear when and from where he developed the idea that the government could use deficit fiscal spending to stimulate demand, particularly during economic downturns." I will revisit the topic by exploring Takahashi's early career development and the origins of his thoughts on economic policy.

Takahashi's thoughts and actions and their consequences contain many valuable historical lessons for today. Which part of his policy package brought about an economic recovery? Where did the conceptual framework for his policy come from? Why did he have to be killed? Was there any alternative? His innovative ideas may give us hints for dealing with the global economic downturn under COVID-19, the confrontation between the United Stated and China, and the domestic political instability in many parts of the world. Constraints he faced may show us the nature of structural impediments, which are common even today. The background to his assassination may reveal the origins of terrorism. While recognizing that we should not expect easy answers from historical experience, I will, nevertheless, explore Takahashi's experience over a long timeframe, from the late nineteenth century, in a global context, and from political, social, and economic perspectives.

1.2 The Scope of This Book

This book is an attempt to paint an overview of Takahashi's economic policies in the early 1930s. To this end, I shed light on the following points: (1) the kind of challenges Takahashi faced, (2) the economic and social consequences of his policies, and (3) the underlying economic thoughts behind his intensions and actions.

To explore (1) the challenges Takahashi faced, we need to investigate the social and political constellations and the interactions among various interest groups, as well as the economic and social conditions that formed the backdrop to his policies. He did not, after all, live in sterile laboratory conditions. He had to deal with power politics among various players with conflicting views and motivations amidst ever-changing external circumstances and rapid social and economic changes. I will review the existing literature in the fields of political, social, as well as economic history, focusing on constraints and potentials for contemporary policymakers.

To explore (2) the economic and social consequences of his policies, I will employ a critical survey of previous empirical works, including my own. Recent developments in economic history, with the introduction of quantitative methods, have brought new evaluations of and insights into the effects of Takahashi's economic policies. Again, recent studies in political history have been rediscovering the various options considered behind the scenes but not implemented. Looking into why a parallel world was not realized, we may be able to see the political economy of his program from a broader perspective.

To understand (3) the underlying economic thoughts behind Takahashi's intentions and actions, we need to study his biographies, focusing on his education. Though he never officially attended school, Takahashi learned from written materials both in Japanese and English, from mentors in a broader sense, as well as on the job in his various positions. Before he reached the age of 80, he had a clear image of the working mechanisms of the national economy and the goals of economic policy and of the nation state. It is important to view the world from his perspective as he formulated his policy package in the midst of crisis. I will, therefore, scan his biographies, publications, and correspondences in an effort to reconstruct his central ideas as derived from his experiences.

The structure of the book is as follows. Chapter 2 overviews modern Japanese economic history with reference to Japan's position in the global economy and shows macroeconomic performance and policy responses in the 1930s. Chapter 3 explores Takahashi's policies focusing on policy innovations in exchange rate, fiscal, and monetary policies. Chapter 4 revisits his struggle with the pressure to expand military expenditure from the perspective of fiscal policy governance and public debt management. Chapter 5 explores the origins of Takahashi's policies by tracing the history of his career and the network of personal connections he made during the course of it, both in Japan and abroad. Chapter 6 concludes with lessons for today.

References

Bank of Japan. 1984. *Nippon ginkō hyaknen shi* (The first hundred years of the Bank of Japan), 4. Tokyo: Bank of Japan.

Bernanke, Ben S. 2003. Remarks by Governor Ben S. Bernanke, before the Japan Society of Monetary Economics, Tokyo, Japan, May 31, 2003. www.federalreserve.gov/boarddocs/speeches/2003/20030531/default.htm (Accessed on November 22, 2020).

Cha, Myung Soo. 2003. Did Takahashi Korekiyo rescue Japan from the great depression? *Journal of Economic History* 63: 127–144.

Eichengreen, Barry. 1992. *Golden fetters: the gold standard and the great depression, 1919–1939*. New York: Oxford University Press.

Flath, David. 2005. *The Japanese economy*, 2nd ed. New York: Oxford University Press.

Fukao, Kyōji, Naofumi Nakamura, and Masaki Nakabayashi. 2017. *Nihon keizai no rekishi (A history of Japanese economy), 4*. Tokyo: Iwanami shoten.

Gordon, Andrew. 1991. *Labor and imperial democracy in prewar Japan*. Berkeley: University of California Press.

Inoue, Toshikazu. 2012. *Seiyūkai to Minseitō* (the Seiyūkai and the Minseitō), Tokyo: Chūkō Shinsho.

James, Harold. 2001. *The end of globalization: lessons from the Great Depression*. Cambridge, MA: Harvard University Press.

Kindleberger, Charles P. 1973. *The world in depression, 1929–1939*. Berkeley and Los Angeles: University of California Press.

Metzler, Mark. 2006. *Lever of empire: the international gold standard and the crisis of liberalism in prewar Japan*. Berkeley and Los Angeles: University of California Press.

Nakamura, Takafusa. 1983. *Economic growth in prewar Japan*. New Haven, CT and London: Yale University Press.

Nakamura, Takafusa, and Kōnosuke Odaka 1999. The inter-war period: 1914–37, an overview. Nakamura, Takafusa, and Kōnosuke Odaka. *The economic history of Japan: 1600–1990, 3, Dual structure*. New York: Oxford University Press, 1–54.

Nanto, Dick K., and Shinji Takagi. 1985. Korekiyo Takahashi and Japan's recovery from the great depression. *American Economic Review* 75 (2): 369–374.

Patrick, Hugh. 1971. The economic muddle of the 1920s. Morley, James William ed. *Dilemmas of growth in prewar Japan*. Princeton, NJ: Princeton University Press: 211–266.

Shibamoto, Masahiko, and Masato Shizume. 2014. Exchange rate adjustment, monetary policy and fiscal stimulus in Japan's escape from the Great Depression. *Explorations in Economic History* 53: 1–18.

Shima, Kinzō. 1983. Iwayuru Takahashi zaisei ni tsuite (On the so-called "Takahashi economic policy"). *Kinyū Kenkyū* 2 (2): 83–124.

Shizume, Masato. 2009. *Sekai kyōkō to keizai seisaku: kaihō shōkoku Nihon no keiken to gendai* (The world depression and economic policy: lessons from Japan as a small open economy). Tokyo: Nikkei Shinbun Shuppan Sha.

Shizume, Masato. 2011. Sustainability of public debt: evidence from Japan before the second world war. *Economic History Review* 64–4: 1113–1143.

Smethurst, Richard J. 2007. *From foot soldier to finance minister: Takahashi Korekiyo, Japan's Keynes*. Cambridge, MA: Harvard University Asia Center, 292.

Temin, Peter. 1989. *Lessons from the great depression*. Cambridge, MA: MIT Press.

Chapter 2
Japan's Plunge into and Emergence from the Great Depression

In this chapter, I first overview modern Japanese economic history from a long-term perspective for the period between the mid-nineteenth and mid-twentieth centuries while putting the Japanese economy in its global context. I then review Japan's macroeconomic performance and policies during the 1930s focusing on exchange rate, fiscal, and monetary policies.

2.1 Overview of the Japanese Economy from the Late Nineteenth to the Early Twentieth Century

In this section, I will review developments in the Japanese economy and society from the late nineteenth century to the 1930s, to give you the background to Takahashi Korekiyo's economic policies in the early 1930s.

After the forced opening of the treaty ports in 1859, Japan pursued the dual goal of establishing a "rich country, strong military" (*fukoku kyōhei*) in order to catch up to the Western powers as an emerging nation state. In the late nineteenth century, leaders of the new Meiji Government adopted an eclectic system based on the domestic version of a market economy from the preceding Edo period (1603–1867) combined with advanced Western systems and technologies. In the early years of the modernization effort, the Japanese government took a cautious approach to external borrowing for national security reasons, namely the risk of colonization as a result of defaulting on a loan (Mitchener et al. 2010a, Mitchener and Weidenmier 2010b). Instead, it determined to improve its current account balance through export promotion and import substitution.

At around the turn of the century, external conditions changed. Japan came to be recognized as a nascent empire and a legally equal partner of the Western powers. Freed from the risk of colonization and having introduced the gold standard in 1897, the government issued massive debts in the international financial markets to fight

M. Shizume, *The Japanese Economy During the Great Depression*,
Studies in Economic History,
https://doi.org/10.1007/978-981-13-7357-2_2

a war with Russia, and Takahashi played the pivotal role in fundraising (Smethurst 2007: 141–187). After the war, external debt management continued to be a key macroeconomic policy issue, and the domestic economy was forced to bear the burden of maintaining and expanding the empire (Shizume 2018a, 2018c).

World War I marked the beginning of stage two of the industrialization and modernization of the Japanese economy and society (Nakamura and Odaka 1999: 12–14, Metzler 2006: 91–111). Far removed from the main battlefields in Europe, Japan enjoyed robust economic growth with a high rate of inflation, posted a current account surplus, accumulated foreign reserves, and achieved massive industrialization and urbanization, even as the vast majority of its people still lived in rural areas. In 1917, following in the footsteps of the United States, Japan imposed an embargo on gold exports. This was an effective suspension of the gold standard. At the same time, Japan claimed its "special interest" in China through its "Twenty-One Demands" to the Chinse government, including the expansion of leased territories and commercial and industrial activities, and the acceptance of Japanese advisors to the Chinese government, the former of which the Chinese government accepted and the latter it refused (Narita 2007: 60–61, Banno 2014: 160).

After World War I, Japan suffered from deflation, financial instability, and economic stagnation through the 1920s, which seemed to end following the banking reforms undertaken in the wake of the 1927 Shōwa Financial Crisis. The reforms included strengthening bank supervision and restructuring the banking sector with mergers and acquisitions led by the Ministry of Finance (MOF) and the BOJ (Shizume 2018b). Prime Minister Hamaguchi Osachi of the liberal Minseitō party asked people to "accept an economic contraction today for the sake of future expansion" when he launched an austerity program in 1929 in preparation for returning to the gold standard. When Japan finally returned to gold in January 1930, it virtually "opened the door to a hurricane" of the Great Depression (Metzler 2006: 217–239). The economy posted a −7.9% negative rate of growth in 1930 and stagnated the following year, suffering acute deflation during the 1930–1931 period (Fig. 2.1). Then, in December 1931, Takahashi returned to office. His policies eased away deflationary pressures and brought economic recovery by attempting to balance resource allocation between the military and the civil economy.

2.2 Contraction and Recovery of the Japanese Economy

2.2.1 Lifting Gold Embargo Plunges Economy into Great Depression, 1930–1931

Before exploring the effects of Takahashi's policy in detail, I will review the intentions and consequences of the brief resumption of the gold standard in Japan.

Japan recorded chronic current account deficits through the 1920s mainly due to higher domestic prices relative to its trading partners. During World War I, prices

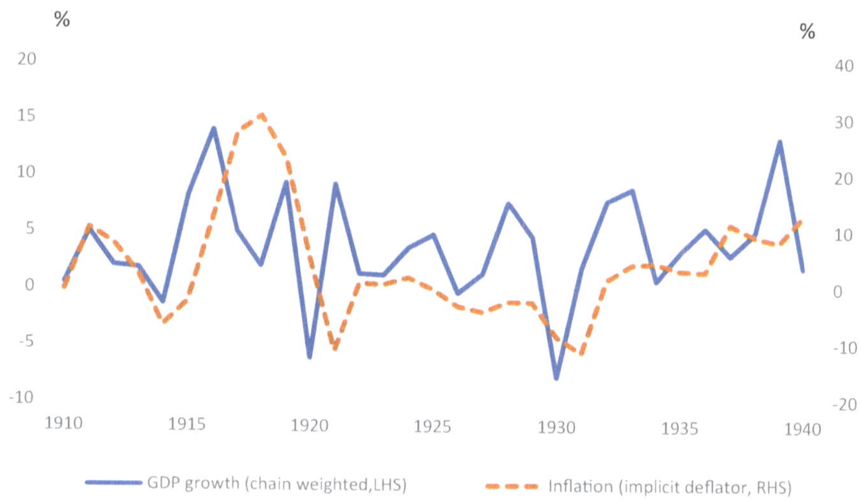

Fig. 2.1 Output growth and inflation. *Source* Fukao et al. (2017)

in Japan soared as high as those in its trading partners, such as the United States and Britain, but did not subsequently plummet to the same extent (Figs. 2.2, 2.3). The resulting loss of competitiveness caused a deterioration in Japan's trade balance

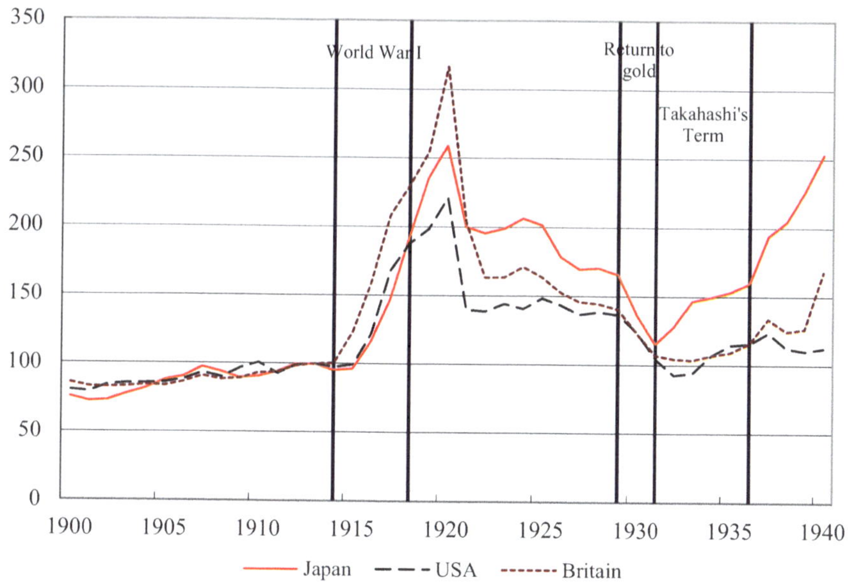

Fig. 2.2 Wholesale prices (1913 = 100). *Source* BOJ, *Hundred-Year Statistics of Wholesale Price Indexes in Japan* (1987); US Department of Commerce, Census Bureau, *Historical Statistics of the United States*, B. R. Mitchell, *British Historical Statistics*

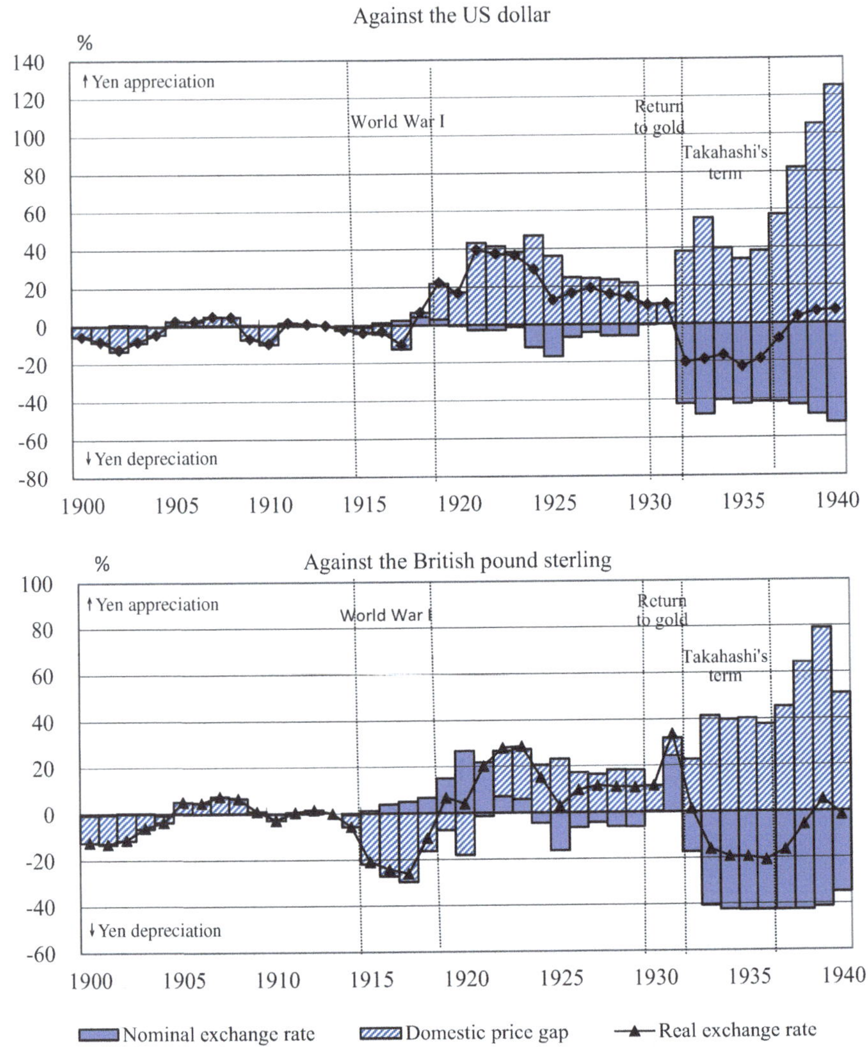

Fig. 2.3 Real exchange rate of the Japanese yen (change from 1913). *Source* BOJ (1987), US Department of Commerce (1989), Mitchell (1988), Asahi Shimbunsha (1930), MOF, *Reference Book of Financial Matters* (various issues)

(Patrick 1971: 225–229). Additionally, Japan continued to have to repay the debts it had borrowed during the Russo-Japanese War (Fig. 2.4).

During the period from 1917 to 1929, when gold exports were suspended, the Japanese government considered lifting the embargo on gold exports several times, at least in 1919, 1923, and 1927, but it either ended up refraining from doing so or was unable to do so due to obstacles until 1930. In 1919, the Seiyūkai Hara Takashi Cabinet considered lifting the embargo but refrained from doing so because

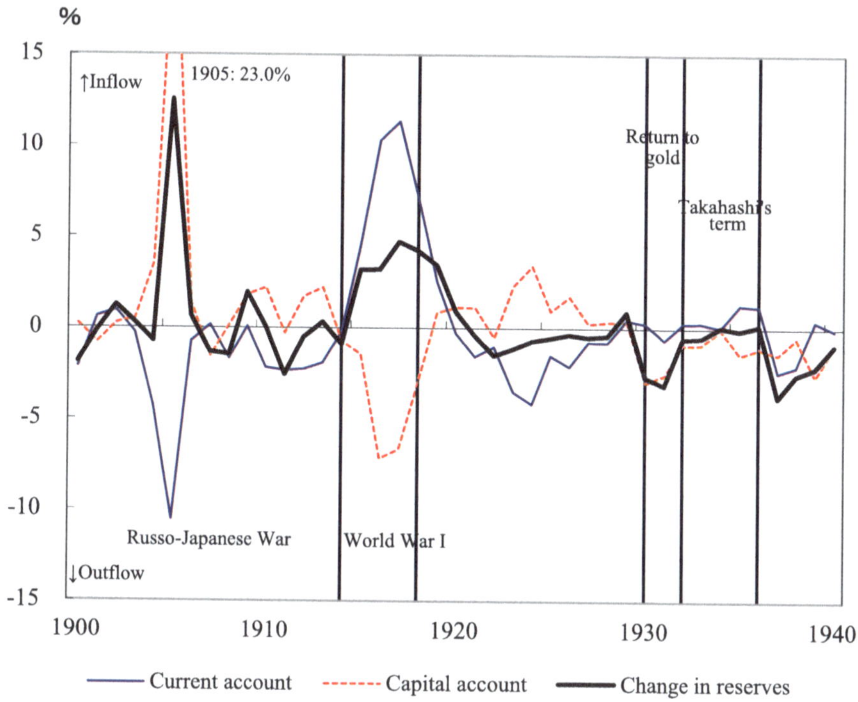

Fig. 2.4 Balance of payments (as % of GNP). *Source* Ohkawa and Shinohara (1979), Yamazawa and Yamamoto (1979)

Finance Minister Takahashi Korekiyo prioritized investing in China over keeping a reserve fund to maintain gold convertibility. In 1923, when the Katō Yūzaburō Cabinet, supported by the Seiyūkai, considered lifting the embargo, the Great Kanto Earthquake prevented it. In 1927, the Minseitō Wakatsuki Reijirō Cabinet's plan to lift the embargo were thwarted by the Shōwa Financial Crisis. These episodes show that restoring gold convertibility had become a national goal, with consensus among political parties. The main question was when and how to do it (Metzler 2006: 193–194; Shizume 2009: 13–14).

When the Minseitō came to power in July 1929, the cabinet, headed by Hamaguchi Osachi, a former MOF official, announced a manifesto titled the "Ten Point Program," a classical statement of the liberal party's policy line along with international cooperation. It included points such as improving relations with China, promoting arms limitation, adjustment and financial retrenchment, balancing the budget (not floating bonds) and reducing government debt, and lifting the gold embargo. The first two—non-interventionist policy toward China and active engagement in naval disarmament—represented cooperation with the Western powers in diplomatic policy. The last three were preparations for and implementation of the return to the gold standard

(Metzler 2006: 200).[1] Inoue Junnosuke (1869–1832), former governor of the BOJ, joined the Minseitō to become the finance minister.

In August 1929, Prime Minister Hamaguchi distributed a leaflet to every household titled "Zen kokumin ni Uttau" (A Call to the Whole Nation) describing the purpose and prospects of Japan's return to gold. He made a speech on the radio, paraphrasing the contents of the leaflet to call for austerity:

> I sincerely believe that, the urgent task for this country is to return to the normality of the international economy by lifting the gold embargo as soon as possible at any price, thereby aiming for a healthy development of trade and industry to promote the national fortune. In preparing for this goal, the most urgent requirement is to implement austerity measures in the public and private sectors to the full extent, reducing prices and the import excess to bring about a gradual appreciation of the yen. We have to accept an economic contraction today for the sake of future expansion. (Hamaguchi 1929)

The move was motivated mainly by three reasons. First, from the perspective of international finance, Japan needed to refinance loans worth 25 million pounds (250 million yen) borrowed in 1905 and due in 1931. It was crucial to succeed in refinancing because, by the end of 1929, Japan had almost exhausted its foreign reserves accumulated during World War I. Key persons in the international financial markets, such as Thomas Lamont of J. P. Morgan and Benjamin Strong of the Federal Reserve Bank of New York, urged Japan to restore gold convertibility to reinforce the credibility of Japanese government bonds (JGBs) with proposals of assistance through stand-by credits (Metzler 2006: 192).

Second, from the perspective of international politics, Japanese leaders were worried that Japan would lose its position as a principal member of the "first class nations" in the post- World War I world because of the lack of gold convertibility (Bryan 2010: 182–183). World leaders, including Japanese leaders, tried to restore world order through what would later be called the Versailles–Washington regime. In principle, the regime consisted of a series of multilateral disarmament programs in Europe and the Asia–Pacific and the rebuilding of the international financial system based on the gold standard (Ahamed 2009).

Japan actively participated in the international architecture of the former: a seat was reserved for a delegate from Japan, as one of the winning powers, in the Paris Peace Conference, and the Versailles Treaty of 1919 and Washington Naval Treaty of 1922 were concluded with Japan's participation (Hattori 2001: 35–43, 91–112). Japan also signed the Kellogg–Briand Pact of 1928, which outlawed war.

However, when it came to the latter, after France's return to the gold standard in June 1928, Japan remained the only major power that had not yet returned to the gold standard while being urged to. During the negotiations for the establishment of the Bank for International Settlements (BIS) in 1929–1930, the designers of the bank originally planned to restrict its board to "countries with stabilized currencies," i.e., gold-standard countries. Mori Kengo, the delegate from the Japanese MOF, negotiated an exception to the rule: Japan would be included as a member on the grounds

[1] The remaining five clauses were achieving a clean government, rousing the people's spirits, enforcing discipline among officials, establishing a social policy, and reforming education (Metzler 2006: 200).

that it was one of the winners of the war and a recipient of German reparations. It was understood that Japan would soon return to gold to keep its status (Metzler 2006: 190, 193–194).

Third, from the perspective of domestic politics, in the late 1920s and the early 1930s, the conservative Seiyūkai and the liberal Minseitō fought each other bitterly under an emerging two-party system of politics with the implementation of universal male suffrage in 1925. At the end of 1928, the high tide of Japan's parliamentary democracy in the pre-World War II period, the ruling Minseitō only held a minority in the House of Representatives. Technically, setting a new gold parity required revising the Currency Act of 1897, which had established the gold standard in Japan, with the vote of a parliamentary majority. By contrast, gold convertibility at the old parity could be resumed simply by an ordinance issued by the finance minister without any formal parliamentary procedure.

Some economists, such as Ishibashi Tanzan of *Tōyō Keizai Shinpō*, proposed a return to gold with a depreciated parity to minimize the deflationary impact on the economy. The proposal, though economically sensible, did not seem feasible under the political circumstances. Inoue Junnosuke, the finance minister of the minority government, chose to lift the gold embargo at pre- World War I parity to avoid political hassle (Chap. 4 of this volume, Metzler 2006: 202).

Finally, Japan resumed gold convertibility on January 11, 1930. In retrospect, returning to gold at the old parity was a policy mistake. If the goal was to restore a stable currency, Japan should have used a new depreciated parity as Ishibashi had proposed and Takahashi effectively implemented later. The option chosen by the Minseitō Government resulted in a disastrous two-digit deflation and acute economic contraction. However, the Hamaguchi Cabinet and the ruling Minseitō won the political battle at least temporarily, achieving a landslide victory in the general election for the House of Representatives in February 1930 with 269 out of 466 seats (Table 4.2). For once, the electorate approved of the Minseitō's liberal policies. Metzler described the moment as "the liberal triumph" (Metzler 2006: 199, Inoue 2012: 102).

Some later observers include the name of Inoue Junnosuke in the list of policymakers who were bound by the "golden fetters" (Nakamura and Odaka 1999: 34–35) as Eichengreen put it in his seminal work. However, Inoue, his fellow members of the Minseitō, and his subordinates in the MOF and the BOJ were not single-minded hardliners obsessed with a myth of the gold standard; they were removed from the enthusiasm for restoring of the gold standard in Europe and properly recognized the risks and stakes of the policy choice. Fukai Eigo, vice governor of the BOJ wrote:

> It is generally difficult to establish adequate standards for monetary control. And even if established, it is difficult to maintain them. The gold standard defines a currency to be exchanged with a certain amount of gold. This constraint sets the extent and the direction of monetary control naturally though not automatically. Even if the discretion of policymakers is defective, the adverse effects will not go too far under the gold standard.
>
> Recently, policymakers need the consent of the public in order to conduct monetary policy. From the perspective of immediate benefits, an abundant money supply may be the best bet both for fiscal and macroeconomic policy objectives; nonetheless, the money supply needs to be properly controlled to avoid future setbacks. It is, however, difficult to persuade

> the public simply by explaining monetary theories or standards for monetary control. The explanation that money should not be issued excessively because it must be backed by a certain amount of gold would immediately convince the public. With the restrictions under the gold standard, policymakers could keep money sound and secure. (Fukai 1928: 302–303, quoted in Shizume 2011: 1132–1133)

Though Hamaguchi and Inoue were aware of the potentially deflationary effect of the move, they may have misjudged its magnitude. The deflation was more severe than they thought because of the rapidly spreading and intensifying global depression. Black Thursday, the New York Stock Exchange crash that took place in October 1929, was regarded as a temporary adjustment at first glance, but as time passed, the events that unfolded were different from what had been expected (Inoue 2012: 99–103). As I mentioned earlier, Japan experienced two consecutive years of severe deflation and contraction and no subsequent signs of economic recovery. Public support for the Minseitō Cabinet waned over time.

Apparently, despite Japan's move to gold in January 1930, investors were not convinced about the sustainability of its external balance because of the huge adjustment cost on the Japanese economy. They, therefore, bet on an early departure from the gold standard. Though the current account was largely balanced thanks to the austerity policies, the overall external balance deteriorated due to continued capital outflow (Fig. 2.4). From January 1930 to May 1931, the Federal Reserve Bank of New York and the Bank of England both lowered their official discount rates several times, going from 4.5% to 1.5% and from 5% to 2.5%, respectively. The BOJ could not follow suit because it had to defend the yen against capital outflows, and satisfied itself with lowering the rate just once from 5.475% to 5.11% in October 1930.[2]

When Britain suspended gold convertibility on September 21, 1931, the flight of capital from Japan accelerated. The BOJ implemented two rate hikes in October and November, raising the official discount to 6.57% in an unsuccessful attempt to stem the capital outflow. The ruling Minseitō was split over the possibility of a grand coalition with the Seiyūkai and, on December 11, the cabinet was forced to resign *en masse*.

2.2.2 Takahashi's Initiatives for Economic Recovery, 1931–1932

On December 13 of 1931, Takahashi returned to office as finance minister and immediately banned the export of gold, effectively suspending the yen's gold convertibility. The yen sharply depreciated against its trading partners, especially the gold bloc currencies including the US dollar, but also sterling bloc currencies. Exchange rates substantially depreciated in real terms to help export industries by making Japanese

[2] Until August 1969, the BOJ's official discount rate was expressed in terms of the daily rate of interest per 100 yen. As of January 1930, the daily rate was 1.5 sen (1/100 yen) per 100 yen, amounting to an annual rate of 5.475% (1.5/100*365).

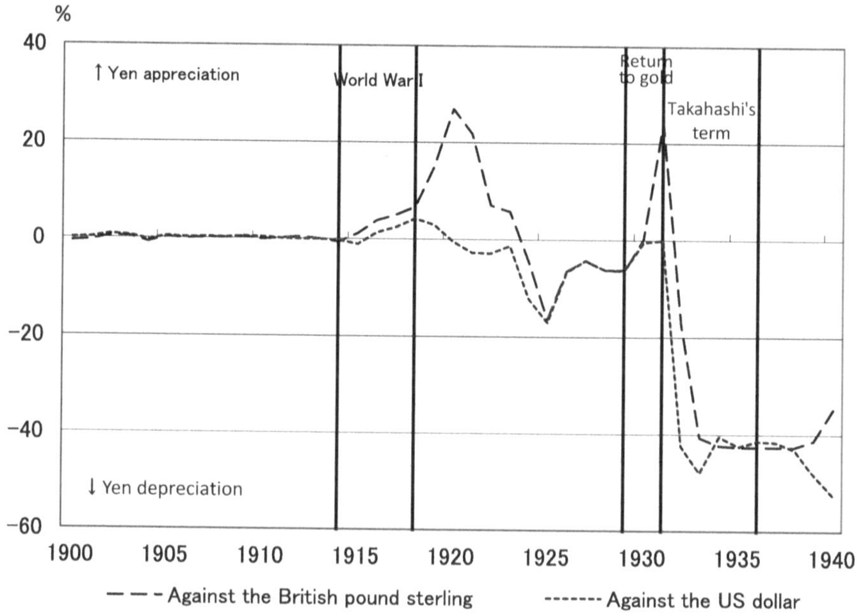

Fig. 2.5 Exchange rate (change from 1913). *Source* Asahi Shimbunsha (1930), MOF, *Reference Book for Financial Matters* (various issues)

goods relatively cheap both in overseas and domestic markets, making exports more profitable (Figs. 2.3 and 2.5).

This exchange rate policy move created substantial space for an accommodative monetary policy. In 1932, the BOJ implemented three rate cuts, in March, June, and August, lowering its official discount rate from 6.57% to 4.38%. In July 1933, it implemented yet another rate cut, bring the rate down to 3.65%.

Takahashi also initiated a fiscal stimulus. In August 1932, a supplementary budget to the 1932 fiscal budget was passed, including a public work program (*jikyoku kyōkyū jigyō*) targeting rural areas that were devastated by the preceding deflation and fiscal contraction. This program and the war expense of operations on the Chinese mainland were financed by government bonds underwritten by the BOJ with lowered interest rates. The issuance of JGBs underwritten by the BOJ started in November 1932 with a reduced coupon rate of 4.5% compared to the previous 5%. The BOJ sold the bonds to other financial institutions and institutional investors, taking into account conditions in the financial markets. On the one hand, this was a policy innovation aimed at smoothing the impact of public finance on the markets, which will be discussed in Chapter 3. On the other hand, it would trigger a fiscal discipline problem when the governance of public debt was lost. The dark side of this issue will be explored in Chapter 4.

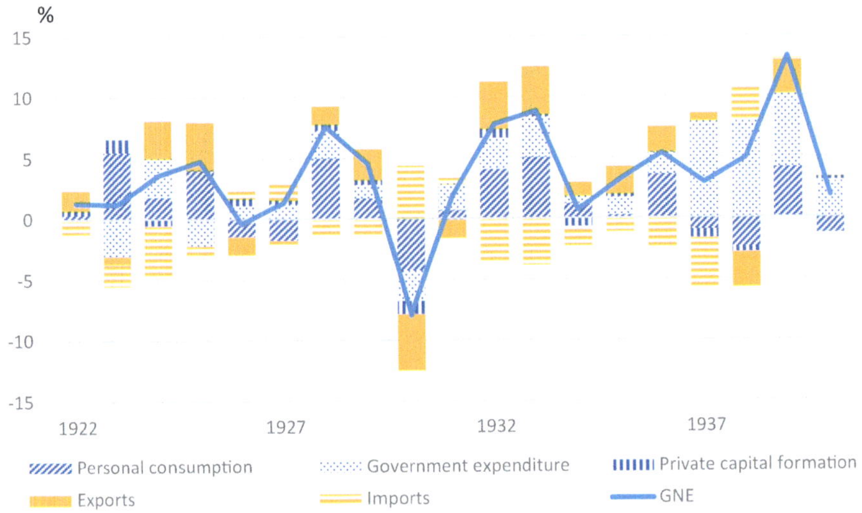

Fig. 2.6 Breakdown of output growth by demand component. *Source* Ohkawa and Shinohara (1979), Fukao et al. (2017)

As a whole, Takahashi conducted a comprehensive economic stimulus package involving exchange rate, monetary, and fiscal policies. The BOJ conducted monetary policy to accommodate the exchange rate and fiscal policies.

2.3 A Quantitative Account of the Macroeconomic Effects of Takahashi's Policies

2.3.1 Takahashi's Stimulus Package and Economic Recovery in the 1930s

Takahashi's economic stimulus package triggered robust economic growth with mild inflation (Fig. 2.1). During his term in 1932–1936, the economy grew at an annual rate of + 5.1%, while inflation was contained at + 3.3%.[3] Almost half (48%) of the growth was attributable to growth in exports, 36% to personal consumption, 29% to capital formation, including private and public sectors, and 6% to government consumption, while minus 19% was attributable to imports, indicating that export growth was the main engine driving economic recovery (Fig. 2.6). The effects of Takahashi's economic policies are qualitatively analyzed in detail later.

[3] According to Fukao et al. (2017), from 1885 through 1940, the Japanese economy grew at an annual rate of + 3.1% and domestic prices (the implicit deflator) rose at an annual rate of + 3.7% on average.

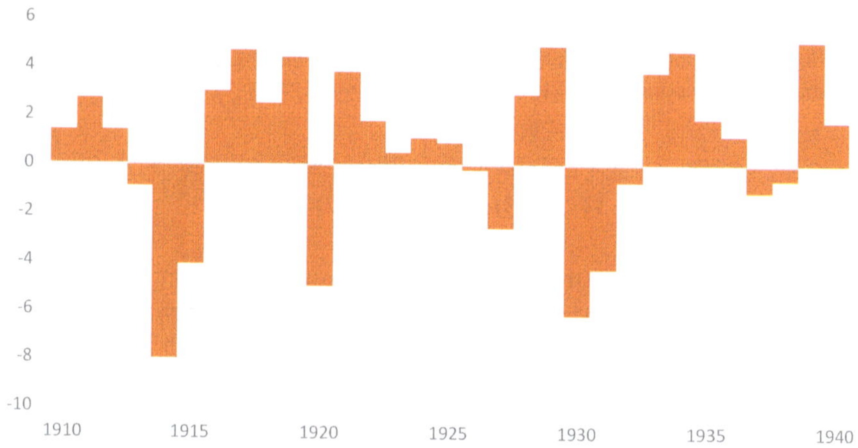

Fig. 2.7 Output gap. *Source* Fukao et al. (2017)

Comparing growth and inflation during the early 1930s with growth and inflation during the 1914–1919 World War I boom years, the annual growth rate was higher during the World War I boom, at + 7.6%, but inflation during the World War I boom was a startling + 17.7% compared with + 3.3% during Takahashi's term.

What were the reasons for such a big difference in inflation between the two periods? There were both external/international reasons and internal/domestic reasons.

First, external conditions differed. During World War I, massive war expenses of belligerent countries created tremendous extra demand for the global economy. In Europe and America, as well as in Asia, inflation was rampant. As a small, open economy, Japan was affected by global inflationary pressures from the main battlefields, even if only remotely. By contrast, during the early 1930s, the global economy was going through the Great Depression, and deflation rather than inflation was the bigger problem (Fig. 2.2).

Second, the output gap, which is the gap between the actual level of production and the potential capacity of the economy to produce goods and services, exceeded 4% of potential output at the peak of 1934. The inflationary gap in 1934 was comparable to that during the peak of the World War I boom (Fig. 2.7). It had rebounded by 10% age points from a deflationary gap of minus 6% in 1930, demonstrating the big push effect of Takahashi's stimulus. The inflationary gap was narrowed during the subsequent years, suggesting that macroeconomic policy management, which I will discuss in detail in the next chapter, may have supported the sustained growth during the early 1930s. By contrast, the inflationary gap persisted for four years during the World War I boom thanks to a non-sterilizing policy of species/capital inflow caused by a persistent current account surplus (BOJ 1983: 451–455).[4]

[4] During Takahashi's second term as finance minister from 1918 to 1922, the government reduced military spending while increasing expenditure on civic services including infrastructure building

In sum, the external threat of inflation was absent and inflation pressures on the domestic front were relatively contained by macroeconomic policy during Takahashi's term compared to the World War I boom.

2.3.2 A Structural Vector Auto-Regression Model

Shibamoto and Shizume (2014) analyzes the transmission mechanism of Takahashi's macroeconomic policy package using a S-VAR model with three state variables (output, price, and inflation expectations) and three policy variables (fiscal balance, exchange rate, and money stock) on a monthly basis. They use the volume of railway freight as the measure of output, the wholesale price index (WPI) as a measure of price, the difference between futures and spot prices of a commodity[5] as a measure of inflation expectations, changes in the financial assets and liabilities of the government deflated by the WPI as a measure of fiscal balance, the effective exchange rate calculated from the export weighted average value of the US dollar, British pound sterling, French franc, and Chinese (Shanghai) tael against the yen as a measure of the exchange rate, and cash in circulation as a measure of money stock.

Figure 2.8 displays the time series of structural shocks on six variables of output, price, inflation expectations, fiscal balance, exchange rate, and monetary policy for the full sample period of Shibamoto and Shizume (2014) from January 1920 to December 1936. Following the authors, the shocks are expressed in moving average for the previous 11 months.[6] The six structural shocks are extracted from the VAR system, to be independent from each other. That means, in the case of shocks on policy variables, not to be induced as responses to fluctuations in other variables, and in the case of shocks on state variables, to be exogenous that cannot be accounted for by contemporaneous fluctuations in other variables. As the model includes expected inflation components, it identifies price shocks as those not anticipated by people beforehand.

The eight vertical lines denote domestic major events, namely, the Great Kanto Earthquake (September 1923), the Showa Financial Crisis (March–May 1927), Japan's return to and departure from the gold standard (January 1930, December 1931), and the start of government underwriting by the BOJ (November 1932), as well as overseas major events, namely, the New York Stock Exchange crash (October

(Chapter 4 of this volume), and the BOJ raised its official interest rate three times, from 5.84 percent to 8.03 percent.

[5] The use of commodity prices for measuring inflation expectations follows Hamilton's notion that commodity futures prices contain some information about people's expectations of price fluctuation (Hamilton 1987). For the baseline regression, they use cotton yarn. For robustness check, they test other commodity prices and obtain qualitatively similar results.

[6] The full sample of the raw data, the identified structural shock data, and the historical decomposition data for the January 1920–December 1936 period is available on the Kobe University Research Institute for Economics and Business Administration (RIEB) website: http://ccss.kobe-u.ac.jp/en/research/database/.

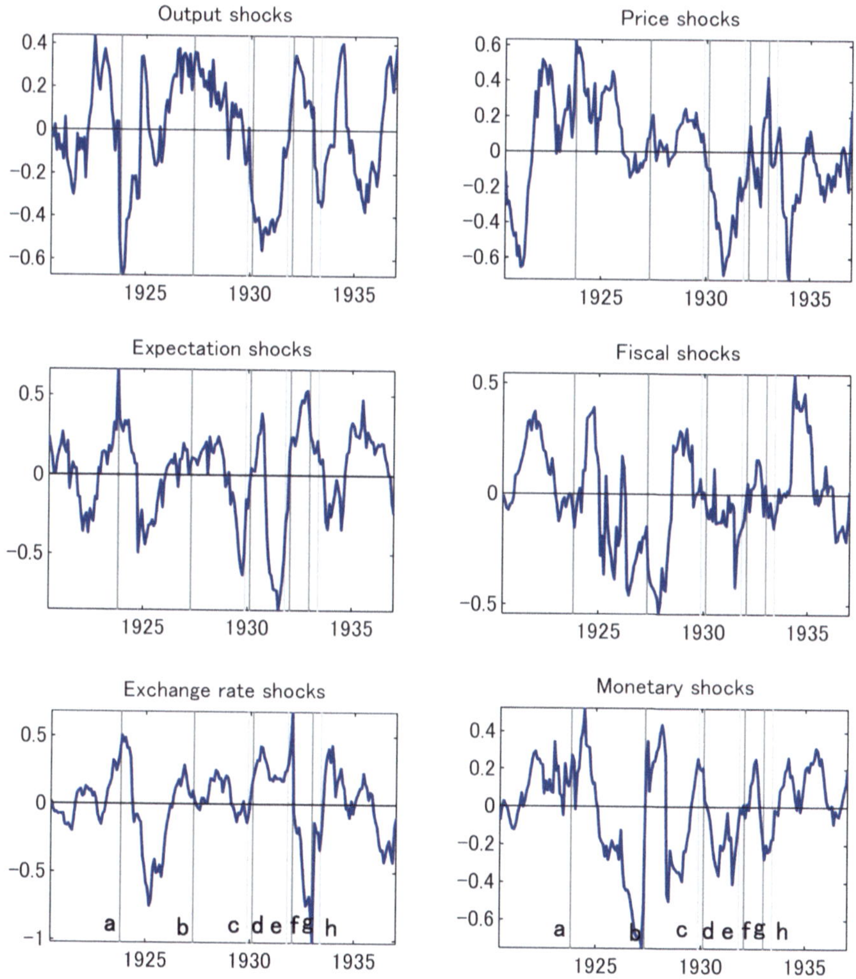

a: the Great Kanto Earthquake (September 1923)
b: the outbreak of the Showa Financial Crisis (March 1927)
c: the NY Stock Exchange crash (October 1929)
d: the Japanese return to the gold standard (January 1930)
e: the British departure from the gold standard (September 1931)
f: the Japanese departure from the gold standard (December 1931)
g: the start of government bond underwriting by the BOJ (November 1932)
h: the US departure from the gold standard (April 1933)

Fig. 2.8 Identified structural shocks. *Source* Shibamoto and Shizume (2014)

1929), the British and the US departure from the gold standard (September 1931, April 1933).

The shocks shown in Fig. 2.8 seem to be consistent with the anecdotal evidence. For example, in the upper left panel, we see two major troughs of exogenous output shocks, representing the Great Kanto Earthquake in 1923 and Japan's return to gold in 1930. In the upper right panel, we see three major troughs in unexpected price shocks during the post- World War I deflation in 1920, during the *de jure* gold standard period of 1930–1931, and after the US departure from the gold standard in 1933. In the middle left panel, we see growing deflation expectations before and during Japan's return to the gold standard in 1930–1931, and an emergence of inflation expectation at around the actual departure of Japan from the gold standard. In the middle right panel, we see persistent contractionary fiscal policy shocks during the second half of the 1920s. The upswing of fiscal policy shocks during the initial stage of Takahashi's term in the early 1930s seem minimal, though not nothing, contrary to the conventional arguments. In the lower left panel, we see major exogenous shocks toward a weaker yen when Britain returned to the gold standard in 1925, and shocks toward a stronger yen right after the British departure from the gold standard in 1931, followed by a surge of shocks towards a weaker yen at around Japan's departure at the end of that year. In the lower right panel, we see major contractionary shocks in monetary aggregates before the outbreak of the Showa Financial Crisis in 1927, followed by sudden stimulative shocks just after the crisis, suggesting massive liquidity provision by the central bank.

2.3.3 The Sources of Economic Recovery

Here, I will explore the dynamics and effects of Takahashi's policies following Shibamoto and Shizume (2014), who employ a historical decomposition analysis, in which the authors decompose the sources of fluctuations in the variables. In this case, we decompose fluctuations of output into six components that are respectively explained by six types of structural shock that are independent of each other: the output shock, unexpected price shock, expected inflation shock, fiscal shock, exchange rate shock, and monetary shock.

Figure 2.9 displays the results from January 1924 to December 1936: the solid line of each panel indicates the component respectively explained by one of six structural shocks on output as deviations from the linear trend, and the dotted line indicates the overall fluctuation of output. The lower left panel shows that exchange rate shocks had significant impacts on output throughout the sample period, especially on the upswing in the output in 1932–1934. The middle left panel shows that inflation expectation shocks explain a large part of the fall and rise in output in the early 1930s. The upper right panel also shows that unexpected price shock had a substantial impact to the fall and rise in output in the same period. The upper left panel indicates that while independent output shocks explain a large part of the fluctuations in output during the second half of the 1920s, in contrast, during the early 1930s, most of the

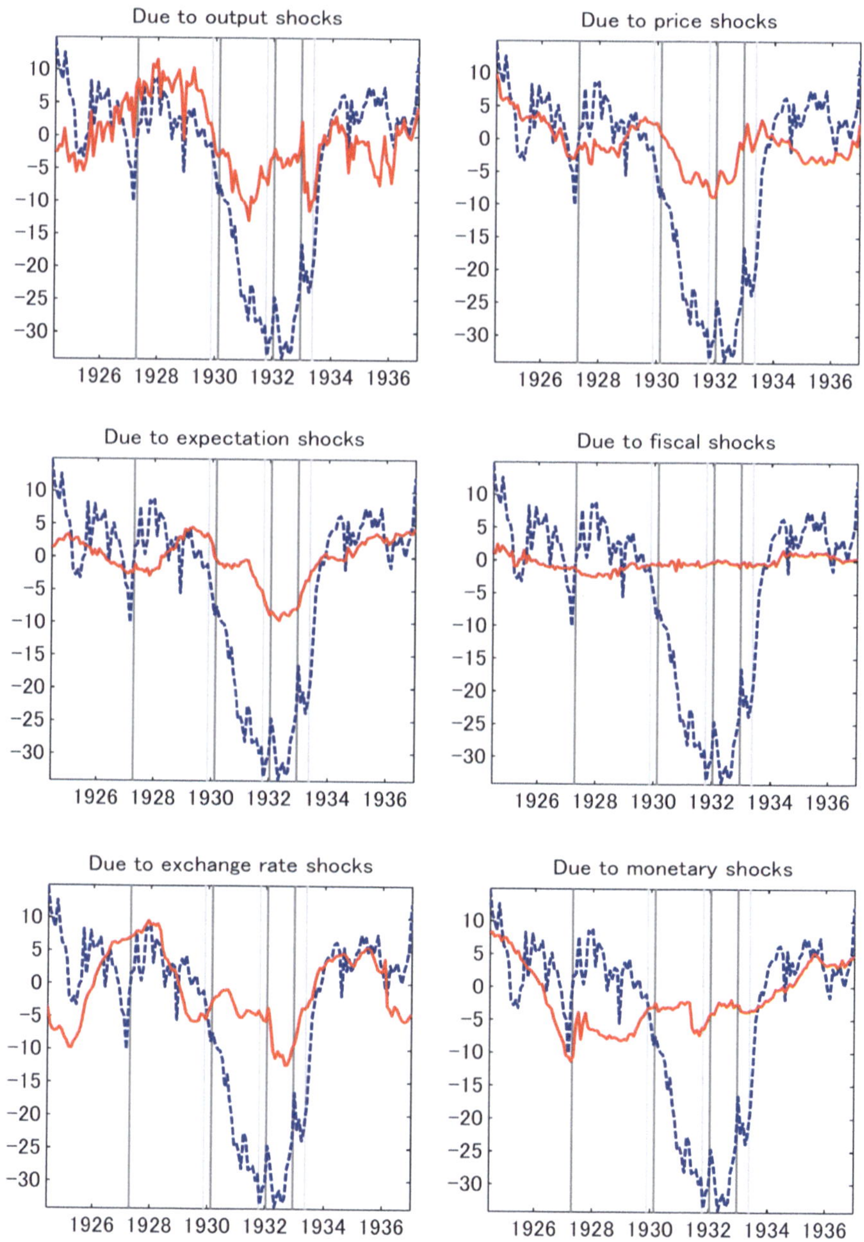

Fig. 2.9 Historical decomposition of output. *Source* Shibamoto and Shizume (2014)

fluctuations were due to factors other than the exogenous output shocks. The lower right panel shows that the effects of monetary shocks on output differed by periods: they had significant effects to ups and downs of the output in the 1920s, had limited impacts during the recovery of 1932–1933, and had substantial supporting effects in 1934–1935. The middle right panel shows fiscal policy shocks had minimal effects on the output throughout the sample period, which suggests that, contrary to the conventional arguments, changes in the fiscal balance played virtually no role as an independent policy instrument during the recovery of the early 1930s.

According to Shibamoto and Shizume, output rose by 39% points around the trend from the trough in October 1931 to the peak in May 1934. The historical decomposition analysis reveals that exchange rate shocks contributed 17% points, exogenous changes in expected inflation 9% points, unexpected price shocks 5% points, unexpected output shocks 4% points, monetary shocks 2% points, and fiscal policy shocks 2% points.

2.3.4 The Dynamics of Takahashi's Policy Package

Shibamoto and Shizume interpret their empirical results as "exchange rate adjustment undertaken as an independent policy played the most important role in recovery from the depression, and expectations played a pivotal role in the dynamics at work." They argue that, during the second half of 1931, speculation on Japan's departure from the gold standard and the inflation likely to follow reversed people's expectation even before Takahashi's return to office and the actual departure from the gold standard. They call the effect through people's inflation expectation the "expectation channel." According to Shibamoto and Shizume, monetary policy was effective, but was not conducted as an independent policy device. Rather, it accommodated changes in other policy measures such as the setting of exchange rates. Their view is that the effects of fiscal policy were limited. In conclusion, they state that "the choice of the level of exchange rate was crucial for changing people's expectations as well as promoting exports and raising domestic prices."

The pivotal role of expectation in economic recovery is confirmed by anecdotes told by contemporaries. After Britain's departure from the gold standard in September 1931, financial market participants anticipated that Japan would follow suit and bet on it well ahead of Japan's actual departure in December that year. What Takahashi did was to make the expected policy a reality (Shizume 2009: 114, 124, Table 3.7 of this volume).

The view expressed by Shibamoto and Shizume challenges a different view by Cha (2003) that emphasizes the impact of fiscal stimulus. To confirm the above result, Shibamoto and Shizume run an additional regression omitting the inflation expectations variable and get qualitatively similar results as Cha (2003): a S-VAR model without the expectations channel suggests effectiveness of fiscal policy. Shibamoto and Shizume contend that the exclusion of inflation expectations would lead to a misspecification and wrong interpretation of the dynamics of Takahashi's policy package (Shibamoto and Shizume 2014: 15–16).

Some observers argue that Shibamoto and Shizume's results overestimate the effect of exchange rate movements and emphasize the impact of investments by Japanese enterprises in colonies in East Asia (Teranishi 2009).

Japan's trade balance (exports less imports) improved by 208 million yen from 1931 to 1935—its balance with former yen bloc (Korea, Taiwan), Manchuria, other parts of Asia, Europe, and other parts of the world excluding North America and China improved by 60 million yen, 434 million yen, 135 million yen, six million yen, and 102 million yen, respectively, while its balance with North America and China deteriorated by 405 million yen and 15 million yen, respectively. Roughly speaking, while improvements in the trade balance with Japanese territories made up for the deterioration of trade balance vis-à-vis the United States, the center of the Great Depression, the switching effect of currency depreciation improved Japan's trade balance with other parts of the world during Takahashi's term. (Fig. 2.10). The S-VAR system employed by Shibamoto and Shizume highlights the switching effect of currency depreciation, while treating the effects of the global Great Depression and the expansion of Japanese investment in Manchuria as exogenous output shocks, with

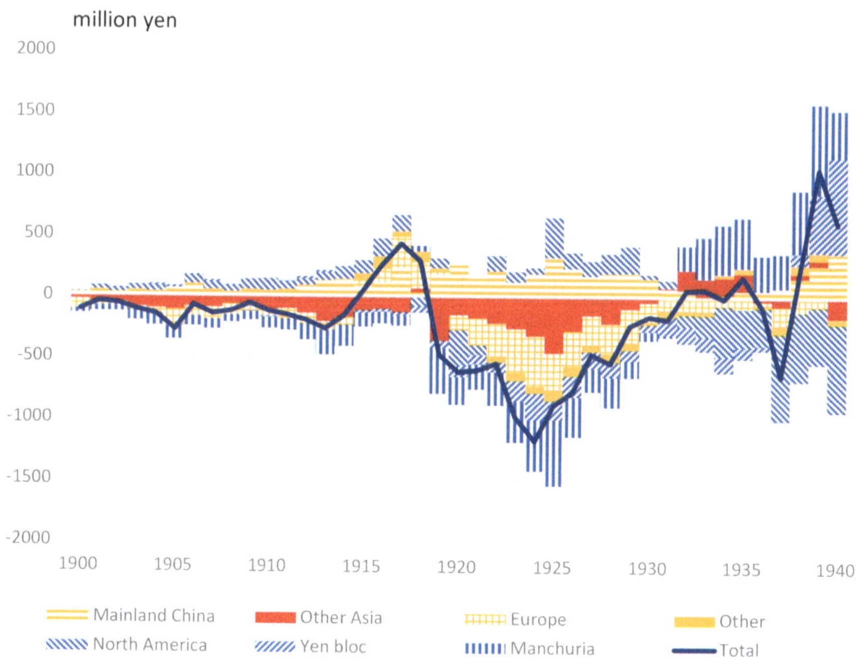

Fig. 2.10 Japan's trade balance by region. *Source* Yamazawa and Yamamoto (1979)

Table 2.1 Fiscal balance, revenue and expenditure of the national government (as % of GNP)

	Revenue (A)	Expenditure (B)	Military	Other	Balance (A-B)
1931	10.2	9.4	3.4	6.0	0.8
1932	9.5	12.1	5.0	7.2	−2.6
1933	9.4	12.2	5.4	6.8	−2.8
1934	8.3	10.4	5.5	4.9	−2.1
1935	8.1	9.9	5.6	4.3	−1.8
1936	8.5	9.5	5.4	4.1	−1.0

Source Shizume (2011)

the former and latter offsetting each other.[7] The Manchurian investment boom and the switching effect of yen depreciation were not contrary to, but rather enhancing, each other to combat with the Great Depression. This is a topic for further research.

Regarding the effect of fiscal policy, Shibamoto and Shizume conclude that fiscal policy did not play a significant role in economic recovery. Using a historical decomposition analysis of the S-VAR model, they show that the output did not respond to fiscal shocks. They also employ a counterfactual simulation analysis, which explores what would have happened to the output in the absence of the actual policy actions. They present that fiscal policy played only a marginal role during the recovery while exchange rate shocks, namely the massive depreciation of the yen, substantially explain the vigorous recovery in 1933 and the high output levels achieved in 1934 and afterwards.

Though, at first glance, the inability of fiscal policy to lift the economy out of the depression seems puzzling, we need to investigate the details of fiscal spending. In 1932, the fiscal balance turned red from + 0.8% of GNP in the previous year to − 2.6%. Expenditure increased by 2.7% points, of which military spending increased by 1.6% points and other spending increased by 1.2% points. From 1933 to 1936, military spending further increased by 0.4% points while other spending contracted by −3.1% points (Table 2.1). The increase in military spending reflected expanding operations on the Chinese mainland including Manchuria and Shanghai in an undeclared war with China. Takahashi initiated a public works program targeting rural areas (*jikyoku kyōkyū jigyō*) in 1932 but had to withdraw from it later to finance the war in mainland China. Overall, the increase in fiscal spending during Takahashi's

[7] The United States departed from the gold standard in April 1933. The Chinese monetary system was complex, but suffice it to say that China was on the silver standard until its November 1935 currency reform (Shiroyama 2009, Horesh 2012). When Manchukuo was established in 1932, it inherited the previous monetary standard and then linked its currency to the Japanese yen in 1934 to become part of the yen bloc (Yasutomi 1997). The yen's depreciation may have had a switching effect on trade with non-yen-bloc regions including the United States and China and alleviated the adverse income effect of the Great Depression.

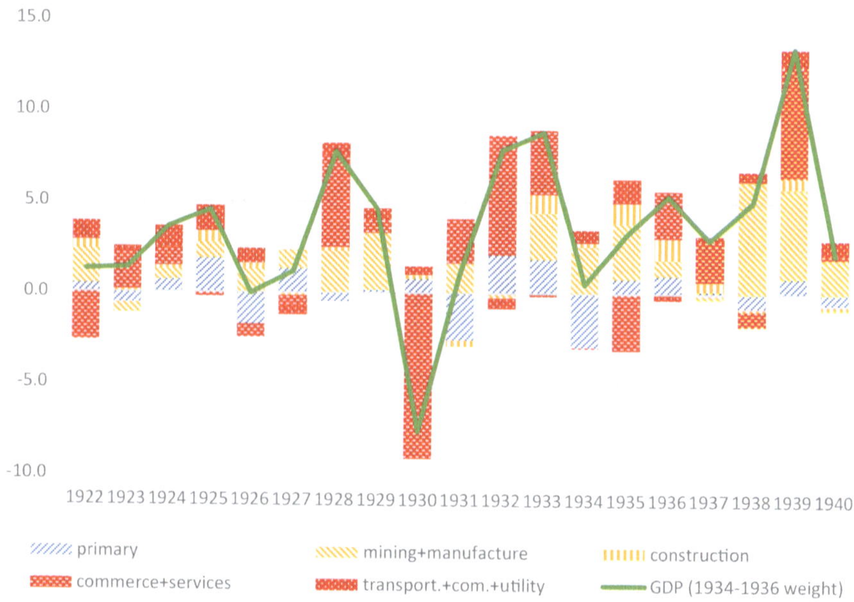

Fig. 2.11 Annual % change in GDP and its breakdown by industry. *Source* Fukao et al. (2017)

term centered on overseas military operations with a smaller multiplier effect than domestic civil spending, which had a larger multiplier effect.[8]

2.3.5 *Economic Growth and Job Creation by Sector*

In this section, I take a look at the economic consequences of Takahashi's policy package. To do so, I review the new dataset of the Japanese macroeconomy compiled by Fukao et al. (2017), which includes GDP and the number of workers by industry.

According to Fukao et al. (2017), the Japanese economy grew at an annual rate of + 5.1% during Takahashi's term in 1932–1936, of which, + 2.0% points was attributable to mining and manufacturing, + 1.9% points to commerce and services, + 0.8% points to construction, + 0.6% points to primary industries, and + 0.2% points to transportation, communications, and utilities, indicating that the lion's share of the growth was attributable to the manufacturing and commercial sectors (Fig. 2.11). This is plausible because exports, boosted by the weak yen, investments, led by low interest rates and the Manchurian boom, were the engines of growth. The weak yen and low interest rates were attributable to Takahashi's policies.

[8] Crafts and Mills (2013) show that the fiscal multiplier in Britain during the 1930s was significantly less than one. The Japanese case may resemble the British case.

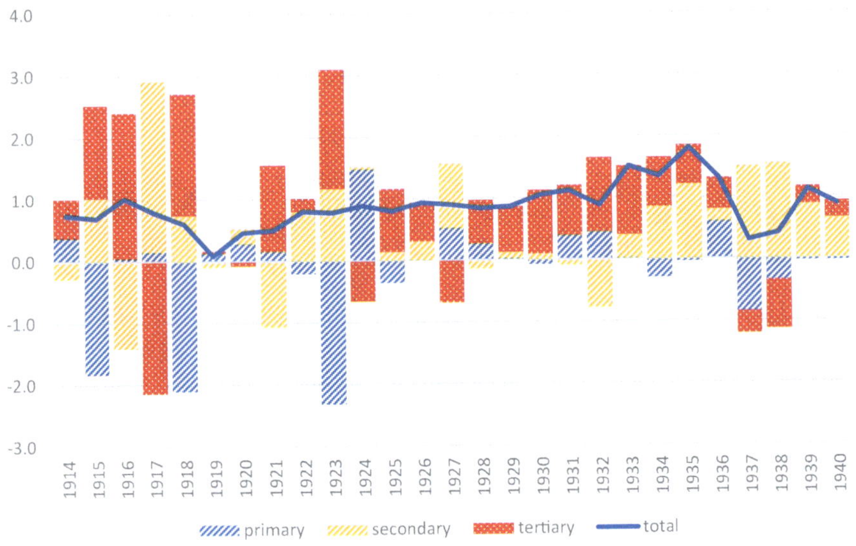

Fig. 2.12 Change in the number of workers (% change from the previous year). *Source* Fukao et al. (2017)

Takahashi's performance was excellent also in terms of job creation. Japan achieved steady growth in the number of workers. Job creation accelerated during Takahashi's term, from an annual + 0.8% in 1920–1931 to + 1.4% in 1932–1936. In the first half of his term, the tertiary sector, including commerce, absorbed the majority of the working population and, in the second half, it was the secondary sector, including manufacturing, that did so (Fig. 2.12).

Figure 2.13 explores Takahashi's job creation in more detail by providing a breakdown of changes in the number of workers by industry from 1931 to 1936. During this period, the tertiary sector created the majority of new jobs—the increase in the number of workers by sector was 228 k for the primary sector, 578 k for the secondary sector, and 1,302 k for the tertiary sector. Commerce was one of the biggest contributors, adding 598 k jobs, followed by machinery at 281 k jobs, spinning and clothing at 199 k jobs, while the military added 210 k jobs and public services excluding the military and education added 219 k jobs. This distribution of new jobs is largely consistent with the theory of an export-led recovery centered on the civilian sector, although the military also contributed to job creation to some extent.

This period saw the beginning of changes in lifestyles and the transition toward a mass consumer society, which would have continued through to the post- World War II high growth period had Japan not headed to war (Nakamura and Odaka 1999: 46).

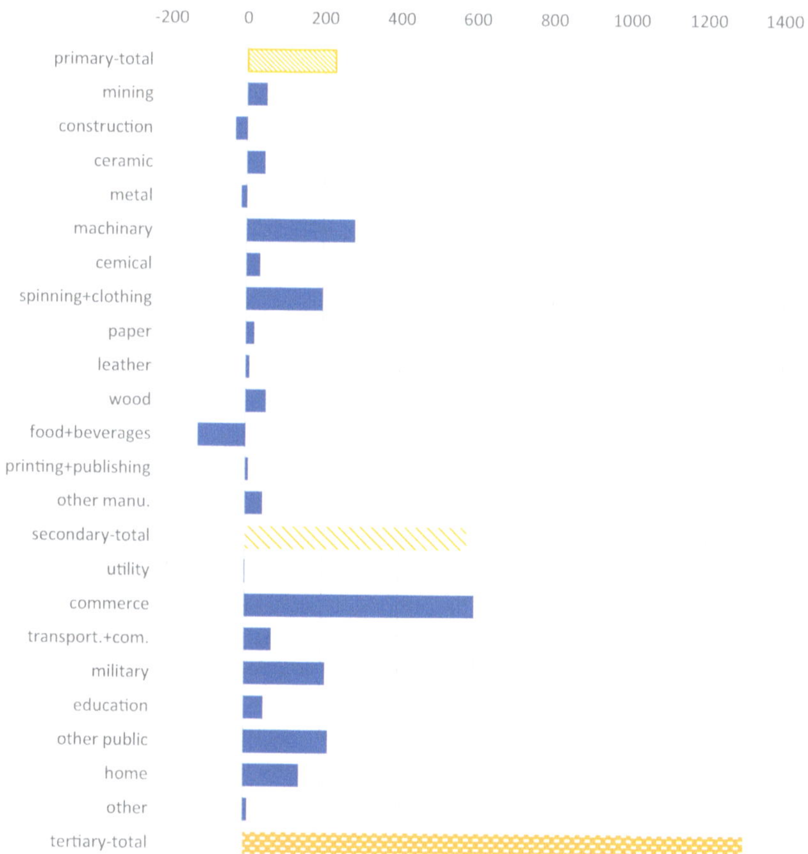

Fig. 2.13 Change in the number of workers by industry, 1931–1936 (thousand). *Source* Fukao et al. (2017)

2.3.6 Distributional Aspect of Takahashi's Policy Package

In concluding this chapter, I would like to touch on the distributional aspect of Takahashi's policies. Fully evaluating the distribution effects of Takahashi's policies will require a book-length project or more, which is beyond the scope of the current work. I will, therefore, merely review the existing literature and examine the macroeconomic dataset recently compiled by Fukao et al. (2017) for future research.

The conventional argument in Japanese economic history is that the Great Depression coupled with the lifting of the gold embargo hit rural areas and relatively poor households in urban areas more severely (Nakamura 1979; Nakamura and Odaka 1999; Nakamura 2012: 149–154). However, how to evaluate Takahashi's policies is a subject that has been debated over the years without ever reaching a final conclusion. Some observers argue that Takahashi's relief program helped devastated rural areas

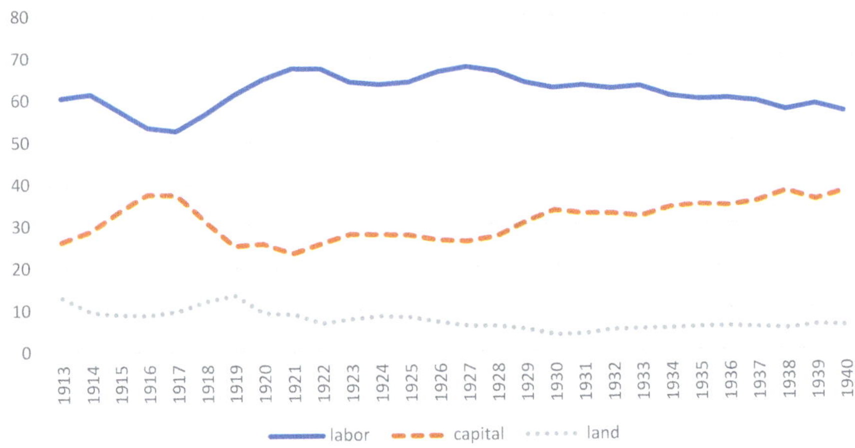

Fig. 2.14 Distribution of GDP (%). *Source* Fukao et al. (2017)

(Smethurst 2007: 264, 267). Others believe that Takahashi's policies failed to narrow the income gap between the rich and the poor. Moriguchi and Saez (2008), comparing the top income shares in Japan with other countries at that time, conclude that income disparities in Japan in the 1920s were roughly comparable to those in other industrial nations, and that "while most of these countries experienced a substantial decline in income concentration during the Great Depression, the impact of the depression on the Japanese economy was far milder. As a result, even by international standards, Japan exhibited a high degree of income concentration at the eve of WWII."

According to Fukao et al. (2017), the share of labor in the GDP peaked in 1927 at 67.7% and went into a decline subsequently. It further declined from 63.2 in 1931 to 59.9 in 1936 (Fig. 2.14). In absolute terms, the labor income increased by 22% from 1931 to 1936 while the capital income increased by 35%. At the same time, income from land increased by 80% alongside the introduction of a system for transferring risks from tenants to landlords in the case of a crisis (Kojima 2020: 127–148, 224–249) (Fig. 2.15).

As a whole, we may say that a large income gap in pre-war Japan was maintained through Takahashi's term, but the poor benefitted from his stimulus policies to some extent.

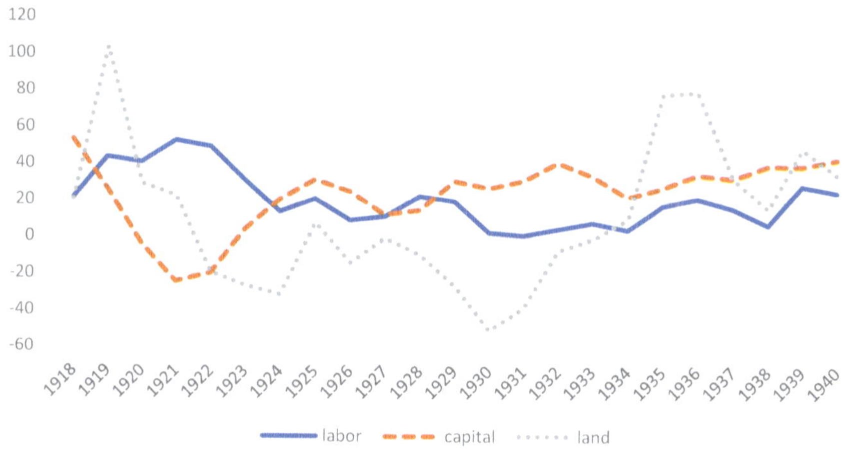

Fig. 2.15 Real income growth from five years ago (%). *Source* Fukao et al. (2017)

References

Ahamed, Liaquat. 2009. *Lords of finance: the bankers who broke the world*. New York: The Penguin Press.

Asahi Shimbunsha. 1930. *Nihon keizai tōkei sōran* (Statistical abstract of the Japanese economy). Ōsaka: Asahi Shimbunsha.

Bank of Japan. 1983. *Nippon ginkō hyakunen shi* (The first hundred years of the Bank of Japan), 2. Tokyo: Bank of Japan.

Bank of Japan. 1985. *Nippon ginkō hyaknen shi* (The first hundred years of the Bank of Japan) 5. Tokyo: Bank of Japan.

Banno, Junji. 2014. *Japan's modern history, 1857–1937: a new political narrative*. Oxfordshire, England; New York: Routledge.

Bryan, Steven. 2010. *The gold standard at the turn of the twentieth century: rising powers, global money, and the age of Empire*. New York: Columbia University Press.

Cha, Myung Soo. 2003. Did Takahashi Korekiyo rescue Japan from the great depression? *Journal of Economic History 63*, 127–144.

Crafts, Nicholas, and Terence C. Mills. 2013. Rearmament to the rescue? New estimates of the impact of "Keynesian" policies in 1930s' Britain. *Journal of Economic History* 73: 1077–1104.

Eichengreen, Barry. 1992. *Golden fetters: the gold standard and the Great Depression, 1919–1939*. New York: Oxford University Press.

Fukao, Kyōji, Naofumi Nakamura, and Masaki Nakabayashi. 2017. *Nihon keizai no rekishi (A history of Japanese economy), 4*. Tokyo: Iwanami shoten.

Hamaguchi, Osachi. 1928. Prime Minister's Address on August 28. Zen kokumin ni uttau (Call to the whole nation). Reprinted in Bank of Japan ed. 1968. *Nihon Kin'yūshi Shiryō: Shōwa hen* (Materials on Japanese financial history: the Shōwa period) 21: 395–396.

Hamilton, J.D. 1987. Monetary factors in the great depression. *Journal of Monetary Economics* 19: 145–169.

Hattori, Ryūichi. 2001. *Higashiajia kokusai kankyō no hendō to Nihon gaikō, 1918–1931* (Changes in the international relations in East Asia and Japanese foreign policy). Tokyo: Yūhikaku.

Horesh, Niv. 2012. *Chinese money in global context: historic junctures between 600 BCE and 2012*. Stanford, CA: Stanford University Press.

Inoue, Toshikazu. 2012. *Seiyūkai to Minseitō* (the Seiyūkai and the Minseitō). Tokyo: Chūkō Shinsho.

Kojima, Yōhei. 2020. *Daikyōkō ki ni okeru Nihon nōson shakai no saihensei* (Restructuring of rural communities in Japan during the Great Depression). Kyoto: Nakanishiya Shuppan.

Metzler, Mark. 2006. *Lever of empire: the international gold standard and the crisis of liberalism in prewar Japan.* Berkeley and Los Angeles: University of California Press.

Mitchener, Kris James, Masato Shizume, and Marc D. Weidenmier. 2010. Why did countries adopt the gold standard? Lessons from Japan. *Journal of Economic History* 70 (1): 27–56.

Mitchener, Kris James, and Marc D. Weidenmier. 2010. Supersanctions and sovereign debt repayment. *Journal of International Money and Finance* 29: 19–36.

Moriguchi, Chiaki, and Emmanuel Saez. 2008. The evolution of income concentration in Japan, 1886–2005: evidence from income tax statistics. *Review of Economics and Statistics* 90 (4): 713–734.

Nakamura, Masanori. 1979. *Kindai Nihon jinushiseishi kenkyū (A study of the modern Japanese landlord system).* Tokyo: University of Tokyo Press.

Nakamura, Takafusa. 2012. *Shōwa shi* (A history of the Shōwa period). Tokyo: Tōyō Keizai Shinpōsha.

Nakamura, Takafusa, and Kōnosuke Odaka. 1999. The inter-war period: 1914–37, an overview. Nakamura, Takafusa, and Kōnosuke Odaka. *The economic history of Japan: 1600–1990, 3, Dual structure.* New York: Oxford University Press: 1–54.

Narita, Ryūichi. 2007. *Taishō Demokurashī* (Taishō Democracy). Tokyo: Iwanami Shoten.

Ohkawa, Kazushi, and Miyohei Shinohara. 1979. *Patterns of Japanese economic development: a quantitative appraisal.* New Haven, CT: Yale University Press.

Patrick, Hugh. 1971. The economic muddle of the 1920s. Morley, James William ed. *Dilemmas of growth in prewar Japan.* Princeton, NJ: Princeton University Press.

Shibamoto, Masahiko, and Masato Shizume. 2014. Exchange rate adjustment, monetary policy and fiscal stimulus in Japan's escape from the Great Depression. *Explorations in Economic History* 53: 1–18.

Shiroyama, Tomoko. 2009. *China during the Great Depression: market, state, and the world economy, 1929–1937.* Cambridge, MA: Harvard University Asia Center, 294.

Shizume, Masato. 2009. *Sekai kyōkō to keizai seisaku: kaihō shōkoku Nihon no keiken to gendai* (The world depression and economic policy: lessons from Japan as a small open economy). Tokyo: Nikkei Shinbun Shuppan Sha.

Shizume, Masato. 2018a. A history of the Bank of Japan, 1882–2016. Jacobson, Tor, Waldenström, Daniel and Edvinsson Rodney eds. *Sveriges Riksbank 350 years: a central bank in a world of central banks.* Cambridge, UK: Cambridge University Press: 328–360.

Shizume, Masato. 2018b. Financial crises and the central bank: lessons from Japan during the 1920s. Rockoff, Hugh, and Isao Suto eds. *Coping with financial crises: some lessons from financial history.* Singapore: Springer Nature: 131–148.

Shizume, Masato. 2018c. Historical evolution of monetary policy (goals and instrument) in Japan: from the central bank of an emerging economy to the central bank of a mature economy. Battilossi, Stefano, Youssef Cassis, and Kazuhiko Yago eds. *Handbook of the history of money and currency.* Springer e-book. https://link.springer.com/referencework/https://doi.org/10.1007/978-981-10-0622-7 (accessed on March 28, 2021).

Smethurst, Richard J. 2007. *From foot soldier to finance minister: Takahashi Korekiyo, Japan's Keynes.* Cambridge, MA: Harvard University Asia Center, 292.

Teranishi, Jūrō. 2009. Book review: Sekai kyōkō to keizai seisaku by Masato Shizume. *Nikkei Shinbun*, August 16 2009.

Yamazawa, Ippei, and Yūzō Yamamoto. 1979. *Estimates of Long-Term Economic Statistics of Japan since 1868, 14: foreign trade and balance of payments.* Tokyo: Tōyō Keizai Shinpōsha.

Yasutomi, Ayumu. 1997. *Manshūkoku no kin'yū* (Finance of Manchūkuo). Tokyo: Sōbunsha.

Chapter 3
Policy Innovation in the Great Depression

Crises bring policy innovations. Facing unprecedented situations, policymakers have worked hard to find solutions and still do so today. Takahashi has often been referred to as one of the world's best policy innovators during the Great Depression of the 1930s. Which part of his policy was innovative? Was that really his work? To answer these questions, I revisit his policies focusing on policy innovation. First, I go through his exchange rate policy with reference to the departure from the gold standard. Second, I explore his fiscal policy focusing on debt-financed fiscal expansion. Third, I dig into the conduct of monetary policy focusing on open market operations. The appendix to this chapter explores the monetary policy operation based on the recently compiled government bond yield term structure data.

3.1 Massive Currency Devaluation

The Japanese yen (JPY) substantially depreciated against its trading partners through 1932. On December 13, 1931, the day of his return to office as finance minister, Takahashi declared a gold embargo, an effective departure from the gold standard. Starting then, he allowed JPY to depreciate against the US dollar (USD) and the British pound sterling (GBP) until the financial markets found equilibrium exchange rates. In November 1932, after JPY had depreciated against USD and GBP substantially, he announced his intention to stabilize the exchange rate (BOJ 1984: 68). After this, the value of JPY stabilized against GBP but appreciated against USD due to the US departure from the gold standard (Fig. 3.1).

In his address to the House of Representatives in January 1932, Takahashi explained the rationale behind the gold embargo and summarized the effects of currency devaluation on the aggregate demand and general prices. He admitted that "the reality of the Japanese situation at the time (on the eve of the gold embargo) had not enabled the government to maintain gold convertibility" (MOF 1965: 400).

M. Shizume, *The Japanese Economy During the Great Depression*,
Studies in Economic History,
https://doi.org/10.1007/978-981-13-7357-2_3

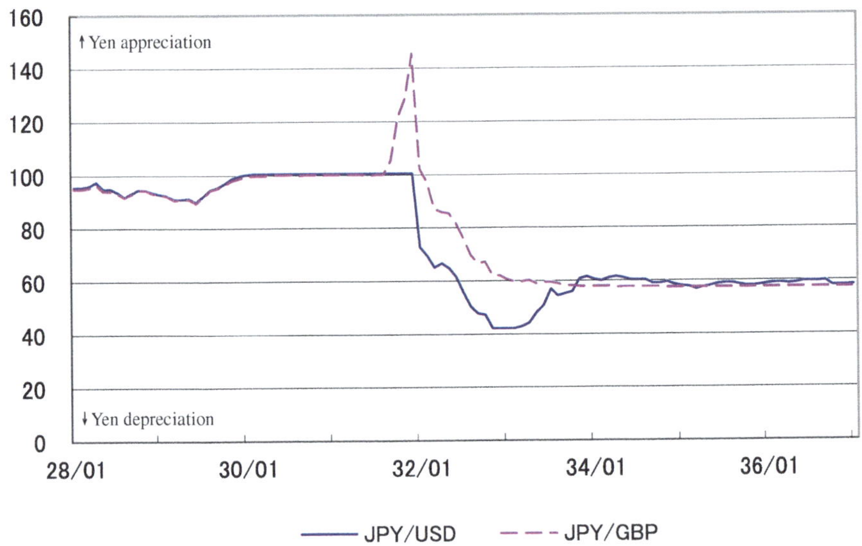

Fig. 3.1 Exchange rates (Oct. 1897 = 100). *Source* MOF, *Reference Book of Financial Matters* (various issues)

He then described the gold embargo as "the first step of the emergency relief plan to help the vast majority of Japanese people escape from the misery of total poverty, to promote industry, and to stabilize the people's daily lives." He continued: "Implementing the gold embargo has corrected the artificial exchange rate to a lower level; prices have been rising internally while falling externally. In a rational manner, this move has stimulated domestic industry and improved foreign trade. These are promising signs for Japan's exit from the depression." (MOF 1965: 403).

Takahashi's comments indicate that he was not bound by "golden fetters"—an ethos of the gold standard in the sense of an outright belief in it as the norm (Eichengreen 1992). He properly understood the transmission mechanism of currency devaluation. This was not new for Takahashi and other contemporary policymakers and economists who advocated currency devaluation as a solution to the depression (Keynes 1925, Ishibashi 1929). However, what was remarkable in the case of Takahashi was his decisiveness in pursuing exchange rate adjustment and his approach of allowing currency devaluation until the financial markets found a new equilibrium.

Contemporaries observed exchange rates and prices both in the domestic economy and in trading partners almost in real time. *Tōyō Keizai Shinpō*, a major weekly economic magazine, published updated gold parity and exchange rates of JPY against USD and GBP, and the wholesale price index in Tokyo, New York, and London normalized to 100 in January 1913. This episode suggests that contemporaries, including policymakers and businesspersons, monitored real exchange rates as a leading indicator of economic conditions. Table 3.1 replicates the process and the results of calculating the real exchange rates of JPY against USD and GBP. Readers

Table 3.1 Comparison of wholesale prices in Japan, the United States and Britain (Jan. 1913 = 100)

	Japan		USA	Britain		Real exchange rate		Value in gold	
	yen	gold	dollar/gold	pound	gold	JPY/USD	JPY/GBP	yen	pound
Jun-29	174.5	174.5	132.0	135.2	135.2	1.322	1.291	1.00	1.00
Jul-31	121.5	121.5	93.0	92.1	92.1	1.306	1.319	1.00	1.00
Aug	119.5	119.5	89.8	91.8	91.8	1.331	1.302	1.00	1.00
Sep	117.3	116.2	87.7	96.0	n.a	1.325	n.a	0.99	n.a
Oct	116.0	114.9	85.5	96.6	77.3	1.344	1.486	0.99	0.80
Nov	116.0	114.9	83.6	97.2	74.4	1.374	1.544	0.99	0.77
Dec	135.0	86.5	81.7	97.0	67.3	1.059	1.285	0.64	0.69
Jan-32	130.1	90.1	79.5	96.4	68.0	1.133	1.325	0.69	0.71
Feb	134.4	86.3	77.4	98.8	70.1	1.115	1.231	0.64	0.71
Mar	128.6	85.1	75.6	96.3	72.0	1.126	1.182	0.66	0.75
Apr	125.0	81.0	73.1	92.4	71.1	1.108	1.139	0.65	0.77
May	121.8	79.1	70.6	91.4	69.1	1.120	1.145	0.65	0.76
Jun	122.4	66.9	71.1	86.7	65.0	0.941	1.029	0.55	0.75
Jul	124.3	68.6	71.8	88.6	64.7	0.955	1.060	0.55	0.73
Aug	141.0	65.1	75.8	91.3	65.3	0.859	0.997	0.46	0.72
Sep	144.0	69.3	76.9	94.4	67.3	0.901	1.030	0.48	0.71
Oct	148.8	63.8	73.6	91.8	64.1	0.867	0.995	0.43	0.70
Nov	156.1	63.0	72.8	91.8	61.8	0.865	1.019	0.40	0.67
Dec	160.7	66.1	71.8	90.1	60.7	0.921	1.089	0.41	0.67
Jan-33	158.4	66.7	69.1	90.2	62.3	0.965	1.071	0.42	0.69
Feb	155.5	64.0	67.2	88.6	62.3	0.952	1.027	0.41	0.70

Source Tōyō Keizai Shinpō

of *Tōyō Keizai Shinpō* easily calculated and compared prices in Tokyo, New York, and London in real time.[1]

Table 3.1 confirms the swift and decisive impact of massive currency devaluation following the gold embargo in December 1931. In August 1931, a month before the British departure from the gold standard, prices in gold in Tokyo (119.5) were substantially higher than those in New York (89.8) and London (91.8), even though prices in Tokyo had fallen quite a bit from June 1929 (174.5). Britain's departure from the gold standard further widened the gap against Britain: in November 1931, London prices dropped to 74.4 due to the depreciation of GBP, while Tokyo prices had fallen only to 114.9. However, once Japan departed from the gold standard in December 1931, Tokyo prices in gold fell to 86.5, while those in JPY (not in gold)

[1] The exchange rate data was updated daily. The wholesale price data was updated on around the tenth business day of the following month. The underlying assumption was that prices in Tokyo, New York, and London were in equilibrium in January 1913.

rose to 135.0. By November 1932, the value of JPY had fallen by 60% against gold compared with November 1931, which was unprecedented, and Tokyo prices in gold hit rock bottom at 63.0 while those in JPY further rose to 156.1. Tokyo prices in gold were at around the same level as London prices (61.8) and lower than New York prices (72.8).

On the whole, massive currency devaluation following the gold embargo restored equilibrium in Japan's exchange rates vis-à-vis its trading partners, reversing foreign trade trends and ending domestic price deflation. Figure 3.2 shows the turnaround in wholesale price and individual commodity price trends at the end of 1931. The biggest cost was not economic but political, and involved a deterioration in Japan's trade relations with its trading partners (Kawakami 1934: 488, Inoue 2011:166–178).

The depreciation of JPY by an annual rate of 60% was not accidental but intentional, and it was well managed so as to be stabilized at the equilibrium level. Takahashi did not intend to trigger a free fall of JPY. On the day of his return to office, he consulted Fukai Eigo, vice governor of the BOJ. Fukai advised Takahashi to take four measures: (1) an immediate gold embargo, (2) the permanent elimination of gold convertibility with an emergency imperial decree as soon as possible,

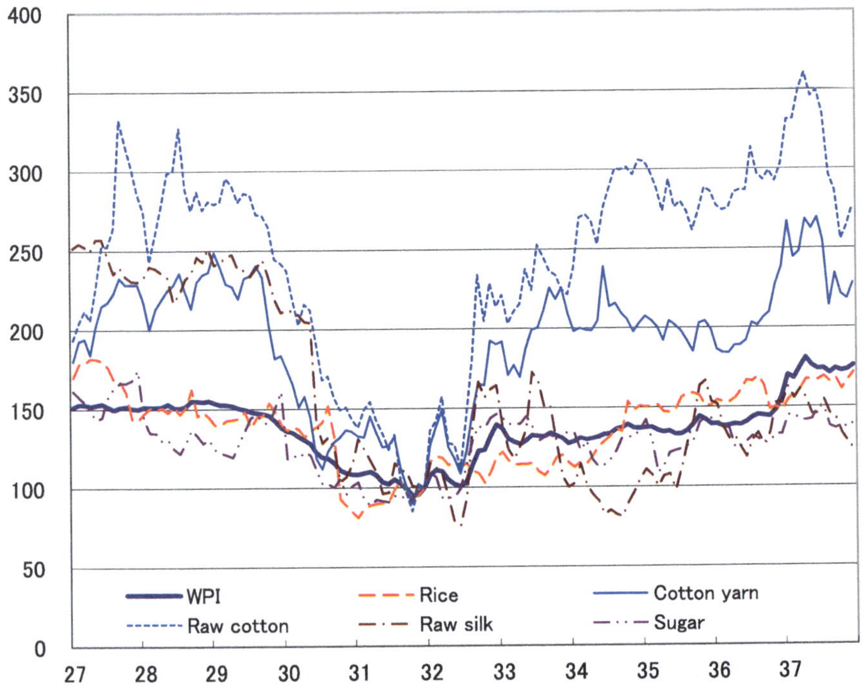

Fig. 3.2 Wholesale Price Index and commodity prices (Dec. 1931 = 100). *Source* BOJ; Osaka Rice Traders' Association; Osaka Commodity Exchange; Yokohama Silk Exchange; Osaka Prefectural Statistics

(3) prudent monetary control to avoid excess liquidity, thereby preserving credibility in the currency and sustaining its value, and (4) the potential need for foreign exchange controls in the event of exchange rate turbulence. Though Takahashi was in complete agreement regarding (1) a gold embargo and (3) prudent monetary control, he strongly resisted (2) the elimination of gold convertibility, and was indifferent to foreign exchange controls. Fukai recalled: "I found it quite odd that, even as he swiftly imposed a gold embargo, Mr. Takahashi strongly insisted on preserving the link between the currency and gold" (Fukai 1941: 260–263). This episode indicates that Takahashi sought an anchor for the value of the national currency. For Takahashi, the gold embargo was a temporary measure aimed at bringing the country out of depression, but he believed that, in principle, gold convertibility should remain as an anchor over the long run even if suspended temporarily.

Takahashi never thought of returning to the old gold parity or allowing a free float of the exchange rates. Instead, he intended a one-time depreciation of JPY to the level at which the Japanese economy's external balance would be restored. And he succeeded (Shizume 2009: 78).

Once the equilibrium exchange rate was restored, the government moved to regulate foreign exchange transactions. In July 1932, it enacted the Capital Flight Prevention Act. Article 1 of the Act stipulated:

> [W]hen the government recognizes a need for the control of the inflow and outflow of capital due to internal or external conditions, it may prohibit or regulate (1) the sale and purchase of foreign currencies and foreign exchange, (2) foreign remittances, (3) deposit transactions, lending, and borrowing in foreign currencies, (4) the sale, purchase, and importation of securities and other types of holdings expressed in foreign currencies, and (5) the provision of credit to foreign residents.

Judging from the conversation between Takahashi and Fukai on the day of Takahashi's return to office, presumably the idea of foreign exchange control originally came from Fukai or some other subordinate of Takahashi, not Takahashi himself. As the name of the Act shows, the legislation was enacted in preparation for speculative attacks against JPY. The Act was replaced by the Foreign Exchange Control Act promulgated in March 1933 and put into effect in May 1933.

3.2 Debt-Financed Fiscal Spending as Part of an Emergency Relief Program

Conventionally, Takahashi's policies in the early 1930s were represented by his fiscal policy. The Japanese expression "*Takahashi zaisei*" literally means "the Takahashi fiscal policy" even though it was a comprehensive policy package including fiscal, monetary, and exchange rate policies, as we saw in the previous chapters.

Until 1931, the Japanese government employed a balanced-budget policy (Fig. 3.3). In 1929–1931, especially, the Minseitō Government conducted an austerity policy to restore gold convertibility, which resulted in a severe depression and deflation coupled with the global Great Depression.

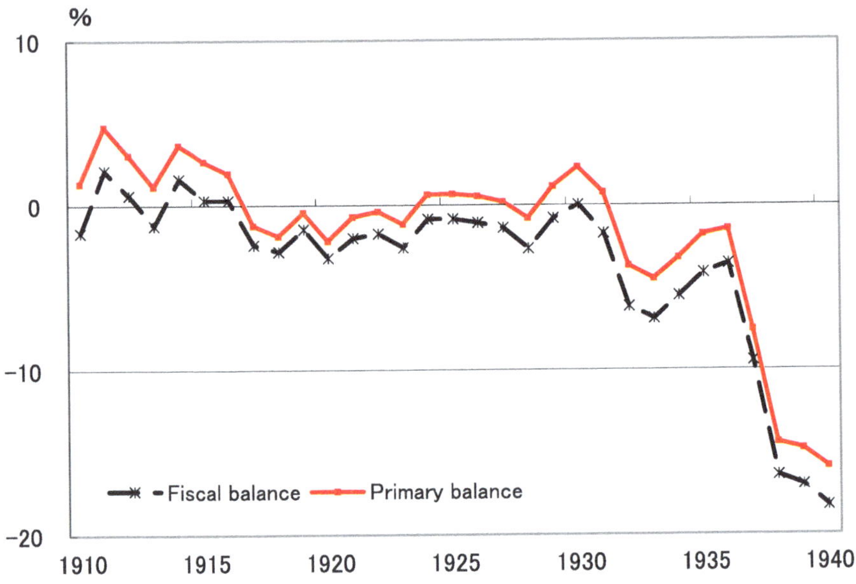

Fig. 3.3 Fiscal balance (as % of GNP). *Note* Primary balance refers to overall fiscal balance less interest payments. *Source* MOF (1936), *Yearbook of the MOF* (various issues), LTES

Takahashi argued that there was no need to balance the national budget every year and insisted on allowing debt financing of fiscal spending. He advocated discretionary fiscal policy using fiscal spending as a countercyclical measure during a recession. He criticized his predecessor, Inoue Junnosuke, for implementing an austerity policy during a depression. The natural choice for Takahashi when he came to power as finance minister, therefore, was fiscal stimulus, which coincided with what John Maynard Keynes advocated for the British government (Keynes 1929).

Takahashi initiated an emergency relief program for devastated rural areas, small and medium-sized enterprises, and unemployed workers (*jikyoku kyōkyū jigyō*). The program was supposed to be an integral part of his comprehensive economic recovery plan (MOF 1965: 132).

After Takahashi became finance minister in December 1931, the Seiyūkai Cabinet led by Inukai Tsuyoshi submitted the 1932 annual budget amounting to a total of JPY 1,327 m for the general account to the Diet. The initial budget drawn by Takahashi's predecessor, Inoue Junnosuke of the Minseitō, was more or less retained by the new cabinet except for a minor revision that involved eliminating a JPY 56 m tax increase. As per both the initial and submitted budgets, the government planned to issue bonds worth JPY 191 m including JPY 123 m for the general account and JPY 67 m for the special accounts.[2] Takahashi stated in his address to the House of Representatives in January 1932: "We have decided to submit a budget that is almost the same as the

[2] Special accounts were set for public enterprises such as the national railways and development programs including in the colonies as well as for financing expenses of war.

one our predecessors drew up because we did not have enough time to formulate a new budget for next year from scratch. At some point going forward, we will submit a supplementary budget with our own new projects" (MOF 1965: 397).

The MOF began the process of formulating the supplementary budget in the spring of 1932 under Takahashi's initiative, but Prime Minister Inukai was assassinated on May 15 before it could be submitted. In June 1932, the Saitō Makoto Cabinet – a grand coalition led by a liberal navy admiral and supported by both the Seiyūkai and the Minseitō in which Takahashi stayed on as finance minister – submitted a provisional budget to the Diet. In the provisional budget, the government added expenditures worth JPY 383 m in total toward military operations in Manchuria and for dealing with unemployment. To finance the additional expenses, the government planned to issue additional bonds worth JPY 529 m, of which JPY 282 m was for financing military operations in Manchuria, JPY 117 m was for the public enterprises and a development program, and JPY 161 m was for general deficit-covering. Takahashi said in his address to the House of Representatives: "The government intends to promote industries and construction with a view to lowering and preventing unemployment" (MOF 1965: 407). In the Diet session, both parties proposed decisive action toward additional emergency measures by the government.

In August 1932, the government submitted a proposal for a full-fledged emergency relief program. This was to be a three-year program costing the national government JPY 600 m. It included construction toward water control, ports, roads, reclamation, military equipment, and shipbuilding, and temporary aid for primary education. The national government would owe JPY 176 m and put a debt obligation of JPY 87 m on prefectural and municipal governments for fiscal 1932. The national government would subsidize the interest payments of local governments. To finance these expenditures, the government would issue JPY 782 m worth of national government bonds. A debt-financed public works program of this scale was unprecedented in modern Japanese history. To forestall financial market disruption, the BOJ would underwrite the government bonds and then sell them according to investment demand from financial institutions and institutional investors (MOF 1965: 410–414). In his address to the House of Representatives, Takahashi said: "Every government has been struggling to find a way out of this global depression, but none has succeeded in finding a solution that can provide immediate results. We have no choice but to try every option in various dimensions" (MOF 1965: 414).

With time, the reality of Takahashi's debt-financed spending deviated from a typical Keynesian scenario. As we have seen, it was initially applied to the military operation in Manchuria and later extended to a public works program. Furthermore, the emergency relief program for rural areas accounted for only 8% of total spending during the 1932–1936 term while military spending accounted for 43% (Table 3.2). Takahashi had to finance war before he could spend on public work projects in rural areas as he wanted.

While allowing debt-financed spending in the short term, Takahashi argued that the budget had to be balanced in the long run to maintain fiscal sustainability. When the Japanese economy began to recover steadily, Takahashi tried to reduce the budget deficit. In his address in January 1933 accompanying the submission of the budget for

Table 3.2 Fiscal expenditures and debt issuance (million yen)

Fiscal year	Expenditure (A+B)	Military (A)	Operation in Manchuria	Improvements in equipment		Other (B)	Rural relief program	Debt issuance
				Army	Navy			
1930	1,558	444	0	0	0	1,114	0	38
1931	1,477	461	89	0	0	1,016	0	120
1932	1,950	702	293	0	0	1,249	264	660
1933	2,255	854	191	114	125	1,401	366	753
1934	2,163	952	164	125	206	1,211	235	743
1935	2,206	1,043	184	120	246	1,164	0	678
1936	2,282	1,089	202	135	259	1,193	0	610
1932–1936 total	10,856	4,639	1,035	494	837	6,218	865	3,443

Source MOF 1955: 4, MOF 1965: 136–137

the following fiscal year (April 1933–March 1934), he warned: "Taking into account the huge gap between revenue and spending and the fact that spending tends, by nature, to increase, we need to make a tremendous effort to balance the budget." One year later, in January 1934, he expressed more specific concern about the ever-increasing military spending, stating: "The revenue shortfall is huge, and the future of our public finances is deeply concerning. The bond issuance amount must be reduced as much as possible. The situation calls for the greatest thrift even in urgent and necessary spending categories, such as national defense" (MOF 1965: 418, 425).

This resulted in Takahashi facing a serious political backlash from the military, which would suffer from a restrictive fiscal policy. The army and navy strongly opposed a reduction in their budgets in the annual negotiation and even demanded an increase. Allegations of corruption with rayon silk manufacturer Teijin were leveled against Takahashi, which later proved false. In July 1934, the Saitō Cabinet was forced to resign *en masse*, and Fujii Sadanobu, a bureaucrat in the MOF, succeeded Takahashi as finance minister. Fujii tried to reduce spending and planned the introduction of a new tax, the temporary profit tax (*rinji ritoku zei*).[3] However, exhausted by the tough negotiation process, Fujii fell ill and resigned and Takahashi had to return to office in November 1934. Takahashi passed the tax increase in 1935 and negotiated for further budget cuts for fiscal 1936, which led to his assassination in February 1936.

The second half of Takahashi's term provide a clear example of the challenges of exiting fiscal stimulus following a recovery, which I will explore in the next chapter.

[3] Although MOF officials started internal discussions on a tax hike as early as December 1932, Takahashi had held back on increasing taxes until the Japanese economy had returned to steady growth (Ide 2006: 150–169).

3.3 Open Market Operations as a Monetary Policy Instrument

3.3.1 Debates on Open Market Operations Before Takahashi's Return

Technically speaking, the largest policy innovation during Takahashi's term in the 1930s was the introduction of open market operations as one of the main instruments of monetary policy, something that had never been done before. These operations were needed to manage debt-financed fiscal spending while maintaining stability in the domestic financial markets. They became possible because of the gold embargo, which created substantial policy space for the central bank, and the central bank was willing and able to employ such an instrument.

Debates on open market operations as a monetary policy instrument date back to 1926, when the MOF established the Financial System Research Committee (Kinyū Seido Chōsakai, hereafter "the MOF committee" in this section) and launched a study of the various aspects of BOJ reform.

Regarding open market operations by the central bank, the Bank of Japan Act of 1882 stipulated that "the Bank of Japan may be allowed to purchase or sell government securities subject to the permission of the finance minister" (Article 16), but there was no reference to the underwriting of government securities by the central bank.

In the draft of its final report in June 1927 for a revision of the Bank of Japan Act, the MOF committee made extensive proposals regarding the BOJ's governance structure, banking business, and banknote issuance, among other things. The report concluded by suggesting the inclusion of "discounting and rediscounting bills issued by the government, and the purchase and sale of national government bonds and securities guaranteed by the government" as one of the regular business practices of the BOJ. This would allow the BOJ to employ open market operations without the permission of the finance minister. The report also suggested not setting a limit for the amount of government securities the central bank could hold. The committee argued:

> [W]hile setting such a limit may be effective in preventing the government from abusing the BOJ for the purpose of fiscal or public debt policy, the proposed legislation would improve the institution and give the BOJ greater independence in its business operations.[4] Further,

[4] The report proposed increasing the number of executive board members from four to six. It also proposed a change in the selection process of executive board members from "all (four) members to be selected by the finance minister from out of eight candidates elected at the shareholders' meeting" to "half (three) of the members to be selected by election at the shareholders' meeting and another half (three) to be selected by the finance minister from out of a doubled number (six) of candidates elected at the shareholders' meeting" (BOJ 1973: 61). The revision was expected to strengthen the central bank's independence from the government. The report also proposed limiting the amount of issuance of banknotes other than those backed by species or commercial bills to JPY 120 m or lower (BOJ 1973: 71).

the legislation would require securities regulation for note issuance, thereby effectively eliminating the risk of excess banknote issuance through holding an excessive amount of government bonds.

The report continued that "in the event that the BOJ needed to reduce market interest rates for the purpose of controlling financial markets in general, such a limit (of the amount of government securities which the central bank could hold) might pose an impediment to its government bond buying operation" (BOJ 1973: 64–66). However, the financial distress in the spring of 1927 prevented the government from submitting the bill to the Diet.

In February 1930, the MOF and the BOJ launched a new study group, the Joint Research Committee on the Reform of the Bank of Japan System (hereafter "the joint committee" in this section). The joint committee continued the discussion in the footsteps of the MOF committee.

In September 1930, the joint committee issued a report with extensive proposals for the reform of the BOJ's banking business. In the report, the committee proposed allowing "the purchase and sale, application, and underwriting of government bonds, treasury bills and other government securities without the permission of the finance minister." The committee recognized government bond open market operations as a key instrument for the BOJ and noted that there was no need for the BOJ to get the finance minister's permission in conducting its main business. At the same time, it argued, "the BOJ has already been engaged in the application and underwriting of government bonds," and "a revision to allow the application and underwriting of government bonds would simply be a clarification of current procedures" (BOJ 1973: 77). Although this notion was technically correct, the underwritings of JGBs by the BOJ before 1931 were mostly for refinancing. By contrast, the underwritings during and after 1932 were for new issues (Takeda 2012: 59–60).

In December 1930, the committee produced another report proposing a reform in the banknote issuance system. In this report, the joint committee proposed limiting the amount of issuance of banknotes other than those backed by species to JPY 500 m or less, including those backed by commercial bills and government securities. The committee explained that this issuing system had the dual intention of "securing the convertibility and maintaining the flexibility of money" (BOJ 1973: 80–81).

In December 1930, the joint committee drafted a bill for the revision of the Bank of Japan Act. The government prepared to submit the bill to the Diet. In April 1931, the committee compiled a supplementary document for future reference. According to the document, in addition to the points above, the committee decided on the policy for short-term credit to the government from the central bank as "from now on, the BOJ's credit to the government should take the form of discounting bills, avoiding the form of lending as much as possible." Pointing to the French case of preferring financial bills over lending to the government, the committee explained that the policy was intended "to avoid abuse of credit by the government and facilitate the conduct of monetary policy by the central bank" (BOJ 1973: 98–99). In the end, the outbreak of the Manchurian Incident prevented the government from submitting the bill to the Diet.

Although the proposals by the two committees before Takahashi's return to office were never realized because of the government's failure to submit the bills to the Diet, the discussions therein paved the way for monetary policy innovation during Takahashi's term (Ide 2006: 59–80).

3.3.2 Monetary Policy Operation During Takahashi's Term

Based on previous studies on open market operations, Takahashi and his colleagues (hereafter in this section, "Team Takahashi") designed a scheme for open market operations and the underwriting of government bonds by the central bank. Fukai later recalled that the scheme would "kill three birds with one stone," namely, provide enough money, facilitate the government's debt financing, and reduce interest rates (Fukai 1941: 269). Fukai recalled:

> During the brief return to the gold standard in 1930–1931, the monetary authorities had to limit money provision as a general rule in order to maintain convertibility. As a result, financial conditions tended to be tight and, in the end, there seemed to be a credit crunch. Meanwhile, advocates for the gold embargo tended to go to the other extreme, arguing for an end to austerity. Mr. Takahashi had been a radical proponent of facilitating industrial development using monetary policy, with little fear of impaired credibility of the currency. However, he came to intuitively recognize the challenge of maintaining credibility through the period of debate on lifting and reimposing the gold embargo. I came to the idea that monetary policy should aim for a balance between production capacity and money provision in order to achieve economic development and maintain stability in people's lives following the departure from the gold standard. This may have contributed to the establishment of one of the principles of his policy. (Fukai 1941: 266–267)

Fukai further recalled:

> Mr Takahashi was cautious in his conduct of economic policy, avoiding abrupt changes. With the promotion of industrial development as his main goal, he devoted policy instruments to the provision of money, monetary easing, and guidance toward low interest rates. However, he avoided giving in to particular demands or providing money in excess for an immediate effect. The BOJ was effectively authorized to independently conduct monetary policy on its own discretion. (Fukai 1941: 267–268)

During his conversations with Fukai, Takahashi often emphasized the importance of the BOJ's close relationship with the financial markets. Fukai replied that open market operations using government securities would be the solution. According to Fukai, Takahashi came up with the scheme of the BOJ underwriting JGBs and the sales of these bonds in the financial markets (Fukai 1941: 269). Table 3.3 shows the BOJ's operations involving the underwriting and sale of the government bonds from 1932 to 1936. The data reveals that the BOJ achieved the smooth absorption of government bonds, managing to sell 90% of the underwritten government bonds to other investors.

Figure 3.4 and Table 3.4 show the growth in banknotes in circulation and its components. Monetary policy during Takahashi's term achieved a moderate but

Table 3.3 The BOJ's government bond underwriting and sale operations (million yen)

	Underwriting (A)	Sale (B)	To private	To public	(A–B)	B/A (%)
1932	200	16	16	0	184	8.2
1933	1,115	843	803	40	272	75.6
1934	701	928	898	30	−227	132.3
1935	751	702	660	42	49	93.5
1936	787	698	678	20	89	88.6
Total	3,554	3,187	3,055	132	367	89.7

Source BOJ, *Abstract of Financial Materials*, various issues

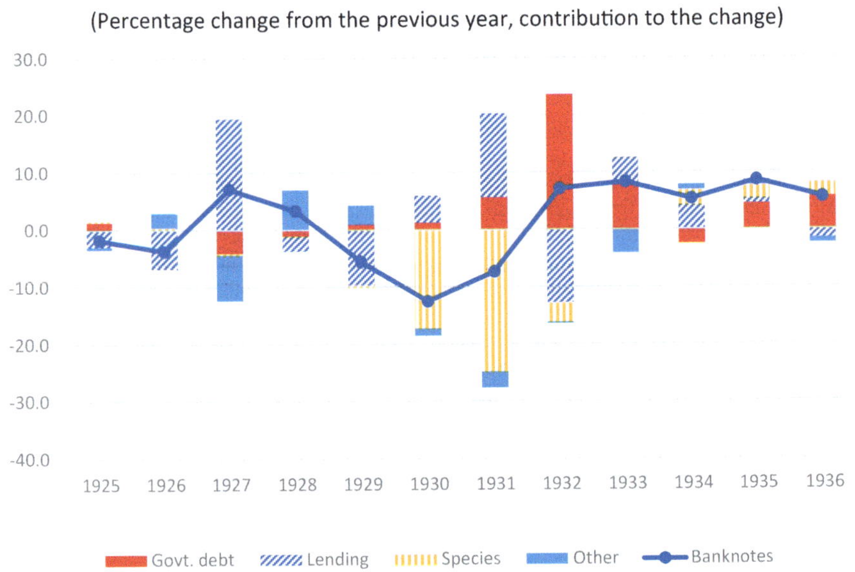

Fig. 3.4 Banknotes in circulation (Percentage change from the previous year, contribution to the change). *Source* Fujino and Teranishi (2000)

Table 3.4 Average rate of change and standard deviation of the BOJ balance sheet items

		Banknotes	Govt. debt	Lending	Species
1926–1931	Average	−3.3	2.9	10.2	−15.9
	SD	6.6	2.9	10.8	10.1
1932–1936	Average	7.0	24.6	-1.2	3.2
	SD	1.3	8.6	6.3	2.3

Source Fujino and Teranishi (2000)

Table 3.5 Credit to the government from the BOJ (end of the year; million yen)

	Total (A)					(Reference)			
		Lending	Financing	JGBs	(B + C)/(A)	JGB total	(D/E)	Banknotes	(A/F)
		(B)	bills (C)	(D)	(%)	(E)	(%)	(F)	(%)
1930	198	25	8	165	16.6	6,029	2.7	1,436	13.8
1931	274	25	89	161	41.4	6,003	2.7	1,331	20.6
1932	610	47	235	327	46.4	6,549	5.0	1,426	42.8
1933	705	25	89	591	16.1	7,821	7.6	1,545	45.6
1934	713	68	275	370	48.2	8,651	4.3	1,627	43.8
1935	845	118	304	423	49.9	9,581	4.4	1,767	47.8
1936	1,013	186	283	543	46.4	10,395	5.2	1,866	54.3

Source BOJ (1986), MOF, *References Book for Financial Matters* (various issues)

steady growth in money in circulation, which was sufficient for economic recovery without being excessive. The annual growth rate of banknotes in circulation recorded an average of 7.0% from 1932 to 1936 while that of real output (GDP) recorded 5.9%. Compared with the previous five years, money growth recovered from a negative figure (−3.3%) to a positive one and its fluctuation was substantially reduced from a standard deviation of 6.6 to 1.3.

The BOJ carefully conducted monetary policy operation to manage the government's debt financing while maintaining the stability of the financial markets as far as possible. Table 3.5 shows the BOJ's provision of credit to the government from 1930 to 1936. The central bank increased its credit to the government fivefold (from JPY 198 m to JPY 1,013 m) and its ratio to banknote issuance fourfold (from 13.8% to 54.3%). As it resold a majority of the government bonds it had underwritten, the BOJ minimized its holdings of long-term government debt and increased its holdings of financial bills. The ratio of short-term credit from the central bank to the government increased from 16.6% to 46.4%.

In terms of interest rate reduction, virtually all interest rates fell through Takahashi's term (Fig. 3.5). From December 1931 to February 1936, the BOJ lowered its official discount rate from 6.57% to 3.65% (−2.93% points). The rate of bills discounted in the interbank market fell from 7.52% to 5.22% (−2.30% points). The yield of Kōgō bonds with a coupon of 5% fell from 5.91% to 4.64% (−1.27% points). Fukai later recalled that "the essence of interest rate reduction was in the reduction of interest rates on government bonds" (Fukai 1938: 365), implying that JGB open market operations played a pivotal role in monetary policy.

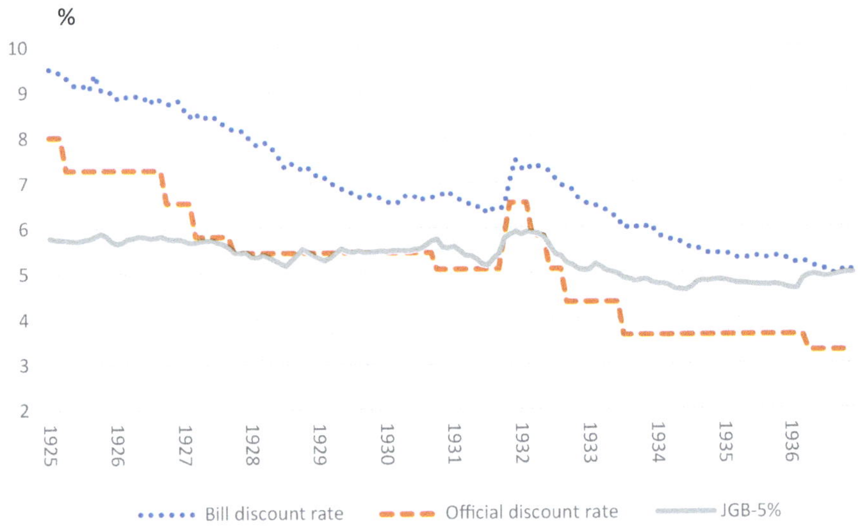

Fig. 3.5 Interest rates. *Source* Tokyo Bankers Association, Shizume (2009)

3.4 Impact of the 1931 JGB Price Collapse on Bank Profits and Debt Financing of the Government

Team Takahashi learned a lesson from the collapse of JGB prices resulting from the interest rate hike to defend the yen and curb capital outflows in the fall of 1931. As the accounting method in interwar Japan was based on the mark-to-market principle, investors with large portfolios of JGBs and other bonds, such as banks and life insurance companies, incurred enormous capital loss due to the interest rate hike and the resulting collapse of JGB prices in the second half of the accounting year of 1931 (July–December) (Fig. 3.6). Among others, two major banks, Mitsui and Mitsubishi, recorded annual net losses in 1931 for the first time in their histories (Gotō 1970: 102–107).[5]

Starting April 1932, the BOJ reduced its lending rate to banks using JGBs as collateral to the same level as the official discount rate (ODR). Under this setting, banks were free from liquidity risks and secured a margin as long as the ODR was lower than the JGB coupon.[6] In July, the Act of the Accounting Method of Government Bonds was promulgated to allow investors to count JGBs by book value instead

[5] Mitsui Bank was established in 1876, while Mitsubishi Bank was established in 1895 as the banking division of Mitsubishi Corporation.

[6] In 1932, the ODR was lowered three times, bringing it from 6.57 percent in January to 4.38 percent in September, while the JGB coupon was lowered from 5 percent to 4.5 percent in November. When a bank borrowed from the BOJ using a 4.5 percent JGB holding, the bank could earn a 0.12 percent interest rate margin. From this time to the end of World War II, the ODR was kept lower than the JGB coupon rate.

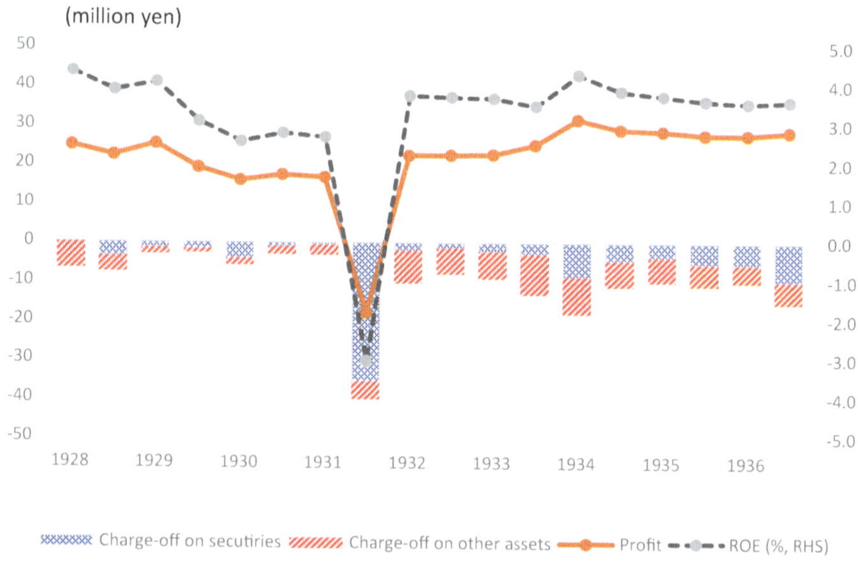

Fig. 3.6 Semi-annual profit of five large banks. *Source* Hirayama (2019: 201)

of market price. And starting November, the BOJ supported JGB prices through the combination of underwritings and open market operations. All of these facilities guaranteed banks and other investors profits from holding JBGs and supported the government's debt financing.

3.5 Concerns About the Sustainability of the Policy Scheme

Team Takahashi employed decisive measures to combat the Great Depression and succeeded. At the same time, they were alarmed at the risk of uncontrolled inflation and the free fall of JGB and JPY prices. They recognized the warning signals through the open market operations.

The BOJ archives hold a folder of documents titled "Documents on Government Bond Absorption Capacity, January 1933–August 1935," in which the BOJ reported on financial market conditions and occasionally estimated the market's capacity to absorb the public debt issued. In September 1934, Fukai expressed concerns about the risks of the scheme in a memo titled "The Opinion of Vice Governor Fukai." He warned:

> The worst-case scenario would be the market's inability to absorb debt due to a lack of confidence in the government's capacity to repay or the fear of a decline in currency value. Once that happens, it could cause tremendous problems for the economic and social as well as fiscal systems. A fear of decline in currency value would induce an abrupt rise in interest rates.

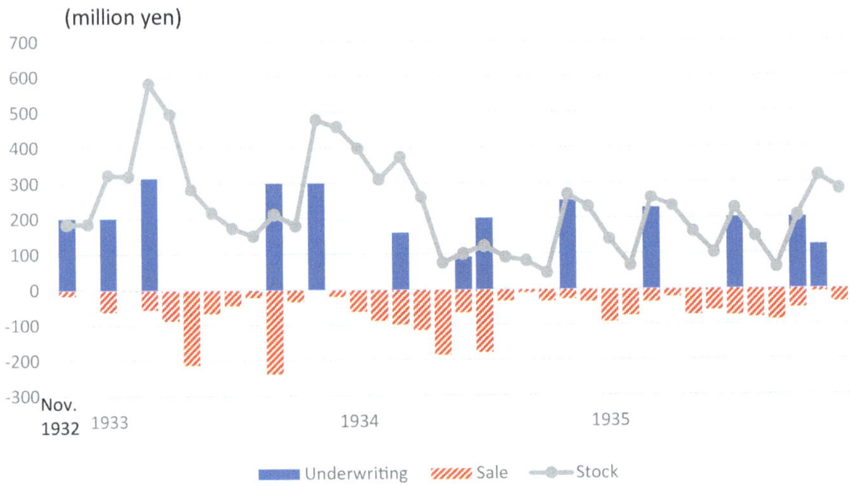

Fig. 3.7 Underwriting and sale of JGBs. *Source* Ide (2006: 180)

By this memo, Fukai intended to advise his counterpart in the MOF, chief of the Financial Bureau Aoki Kazuo, observing the domestic production capacity reach full employment, private investment bounce back, and the market capacity for absorbing JGBs reach its upper limit (Ide 2006: 174–182). Figure 3.7 shows that the monthly volume of JGB sales decreased in and after the fall of 1934. The BOJ received a signal from the financial markets of the difficulty of selling underwritten JGBs. Apparently, Fukai derived his lesson from the German experience of hyperinflation in the early 1920s (Shizume 2009: 195).

In response to the market signal, Team Takahashi made a change in macroeconomic policy. They terminated the public works emergency rescue program to reduce the spending and negotiated on budget reduction with the military, while maintaining monetary easing. The tough negotiations paved the way for Takahashi's assassination and a total loss of fiscal discipline, which I will discuss in the next chapter.

3.6 Appendix: Team Takahashi's Monetary Policy as Viewed from the Term Structure of Interest Rates

3.6.1 Abstract of the Appendix

In this appendix, I explore Team Takahashi's monetary policy from the term structure of interest rates using a new dataset of JGB yields from January 1928 to April 1936 based on Shizume (2008) and Shizume (2009). First, I explain the motivation for constructing such a dataset by showing the existing series of interest rates and the limitations of their utility in an econometric analysis. Second, I describe the data sources and methodology of constructing the new dataset. Third, using the newly constructed dataset, I employ a principal component analysis to explore the behavior of market interest rates in response to external shocks and the implementation of Takahashi's policy package. Finally, I confirm the results with anecdotal evidence based on the views of market participants.

3.6.2 Existing Interest Rate Data and the Motivation for Constructing a New Dataset of JGB Yields

In this subsection, I present the motivation for constructing a new dataset of JGB yields with different maturities by showing the existing series of interest rates and the limitations of its utility in an econometric analysis.

Figure 3.8 shows the representative interest rates in Japan during the interwar period available as contemporary statistics. The official discount rate was the rate at which the BOJ discounted eligible commercial bills from other banks. The Tokyo call rate was the interbank rate at which banks lent to or borrowed from other banks. I take the lowest unconditional rate – "the lowest" standing for the lowest interest rate at which loans were provided, suggesting a borrower with the highest credit profile, and "unconditional" implying that these loans were callable by the lender

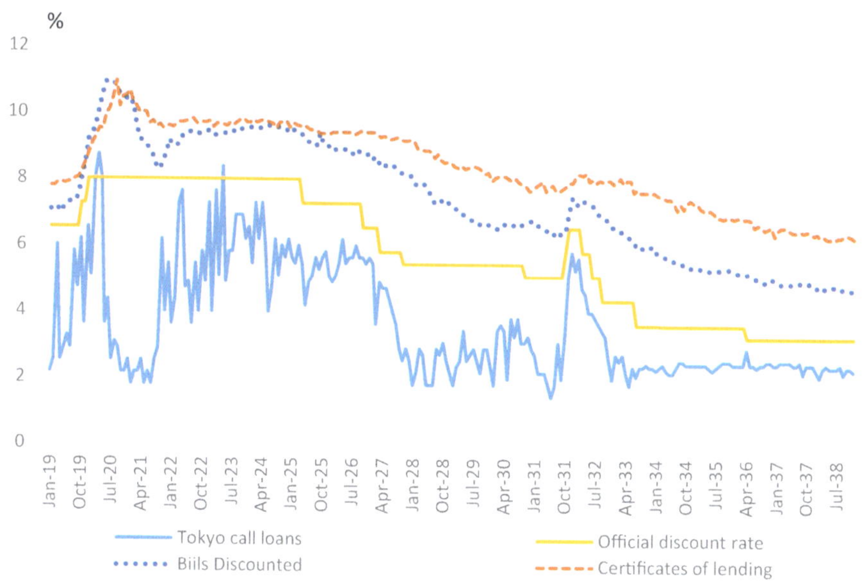

Fig. 3.8 Existing interest rate data. *Source* MOF, *Reference Book of Financial Matters* (various issues)

at any time. The bills discounted rate and the certificates of lending rate were the rates at which banks lent to their customers. The bills discounted rate was the rate at which banks discounted commercial bills and financing bills from their customers. The certificates of lending rate was the rate at which banks extended credit to their customers with a certificate of credit. Bills discounted were shorter-term instruments, and were considered to be more liquid and creditworthy than certificates of lending.[7]

When we use interest rates in research, it is important to choose a rate that fits the purpose of the study. For instance, to understand the cost for borrowers, the bills discounted rate or certificates of lending rate may be the most relevant depending on the borrowers' risk profiles. If the study requires a risk-free rate, say for estimating inflation expectation, bills discounted or certificates of lending rates would be unsuitable, because banks imposed substantial risk premia in the interwar period in Japan (Shizume 2009: 87–93, Shizume 2018).[8] For international comparisons, meanwhile, rates with the same profile should be used (Shizume 2009: 58–68).[9]

During the interwar period, the government issued bonds with various maturities, and a wide variety of investors, including banks, life insurance companies, and individuals, held and traded government securities. In 1931, out of 6.3 billion yen worth of such securities, financial institutions held 2.4 billion yen worth, domestic individuals 1.1 billion yen worth, international investors 1.4 billion yen worth, the Deposit Bureau of the MOF 1.2 billion yen worth, and the BOJ 0.3 billion yen worth (Fujino and Teranishi 2000).

JGB prices were published daily by the Tokyo Stock Exchange (TSE) for the convenience of investors. Traditionally, Japanese investors calculated interest rates using the simple interest method. However, they started using the compound interest method in the 1920s. The Japan Hypothec Bank published aggregated data for the yields of JGBs, municipal bonds, bank bonds, and corporate bonds starting July 1921. The Tokyo Bankers Association published interest rate calculation tables using the compound method starting 1927 for the convenience of investors (Shimada 1928: 118–128).[10]

To further explore the operation of monetary policy during Takahashi's term in the early 1930s, it is important to dig into changes in the term structure of market interest rates. To do so, I construct a dataset of risk-free interest rates from the yields

[7] Aoki (1932) estimated average maturities of each form of bank credit using the volume of credit provision in 1927 and its balance at the end of the year and got the following results: five days for call loans, 43 days for bills discounted, and 230 days for certificates of lending. For a detailed description of interest rate data related to bank credit, see Shizume (2009: 43–44).

[8] Shizume (2009) argues that using the certificates of lending rate to estimate inflation expectations would yield a substantial bias in the result.

[9] Shizume (2009) revisits the analysis of Obstfeld et al. (2004) on the integration of the Japanese financial markets with the international financial centers of London and New York. Using the JGB rate instead of the bills discounted rate, which Obstfeld et al. uses, Shizume comes to the conclusion that the Japanese financial markets in the interwar period were largely integrated with the international centers. The results of Obstfeld et al. using the bills discounted rate contain a substantial risk premium factor.

[10] Shimada (1932) also mentions tables for calculating rates using the compound method, but I have not been able to find these tables.

of JGBs with different maturities and employ principal component analysis following the methodology used in financial literature.

3.6.2.1 Compound Yields of JGBs with Different Maturities

In this subsection, I present a dataset of JGBs with different maturities from January 1928 to April 1936.[11] I use the price data of JGBs listed on the TSE. Quoted prices and trading volumes of each item were published daily. The TSE published a monthly report (hereafter the TSE report) that provided the details of transactions on the floor, including prices and trade volumes for each bond and company stock share. It also included comments on market conditions based on the view of market participants. The information in the TSE report was published in both Japanese and English, and it was widely circulated among related communities including domestic and international investors, policymakers, and academia.

According to the TSE report, 582 bonds were listed on the TSE at the end of 1931, including 38 JGBs, one foreign bond, 95 municipal bonds, and 448 corporate bonds. The floor trading markets were separated into two – the spot trading and futures trading markets. Apart from floor trading, enormous volumes of transactions were executed over the counter of trading members (Shizume 2009: 51).

I choose interest-bearing JGBs, which were listed on the spot-trading section of the TSE, and calculate the compound yield to maturity, r_t, for each bond item. One of the items most actively traded as the benchmark was Kō-gō 5% bond, issued in 1908–1909 and set to mature in 1962–1963.[12] The formula for the calculation is:

$$P_t = \sum_{j=t}^{n} CF_j \bullet (1 + r_t)(1 + r_t(1 + r_t)^{\frac{j-t}{12}}, \qquad \text{(A-1)}$$

where P_t represents the bond price at time t normalized to 100 at maturity, CF_j represents cash flow at time j, n represents the time of maturity ($n \geq t$), and t, j, and n are expressed in months. I use linear interpolation to compute yields for maturities of 1.5, 2.5, 3.5, 4.5, 7.5, and 10 years.[13] I then obtain a yield curve for each period (month).[14] I add the financing bill rate where available.[15]

Figure 3.9 shows the yield curves from January 1928 to February 1936. Changes in the JGB yield curve suggest severe turbulence from the fall of 1931 through the spring of 1932 and a positive effect of monetary easing through 1932.

---

[11] Raw data and detailed methods are available in Shizume (2008).

[12] From 1886 to October 1932, the Japanese government issued all domestic bonds with a coupon of five percent. It reduced the coupon to 4.5 percent when it issued bonds underwritten by the BOJ.

[13] The full sample of the raw data for the January 1928–April 1936 period is available on the Kobe University Research Institute for Economics and Business Administration (RIEB) website: https://ccss.kobe-u.ac.jp/en/research/database/. Details of the calculation are available in Shizume (2008).

[14] Strictly speaking, my calculation of yield to maturity includes the cash flow of interest payment. To calculate pure yield, one needs to separate interest payments and construct a dataset of zero-coupon bonds. In this sense, the data in this appendix are approximations.

[15] Occasionally, financing bills were issued to bridge the short-term gap between spending and revenue of the government within a fiscal year.

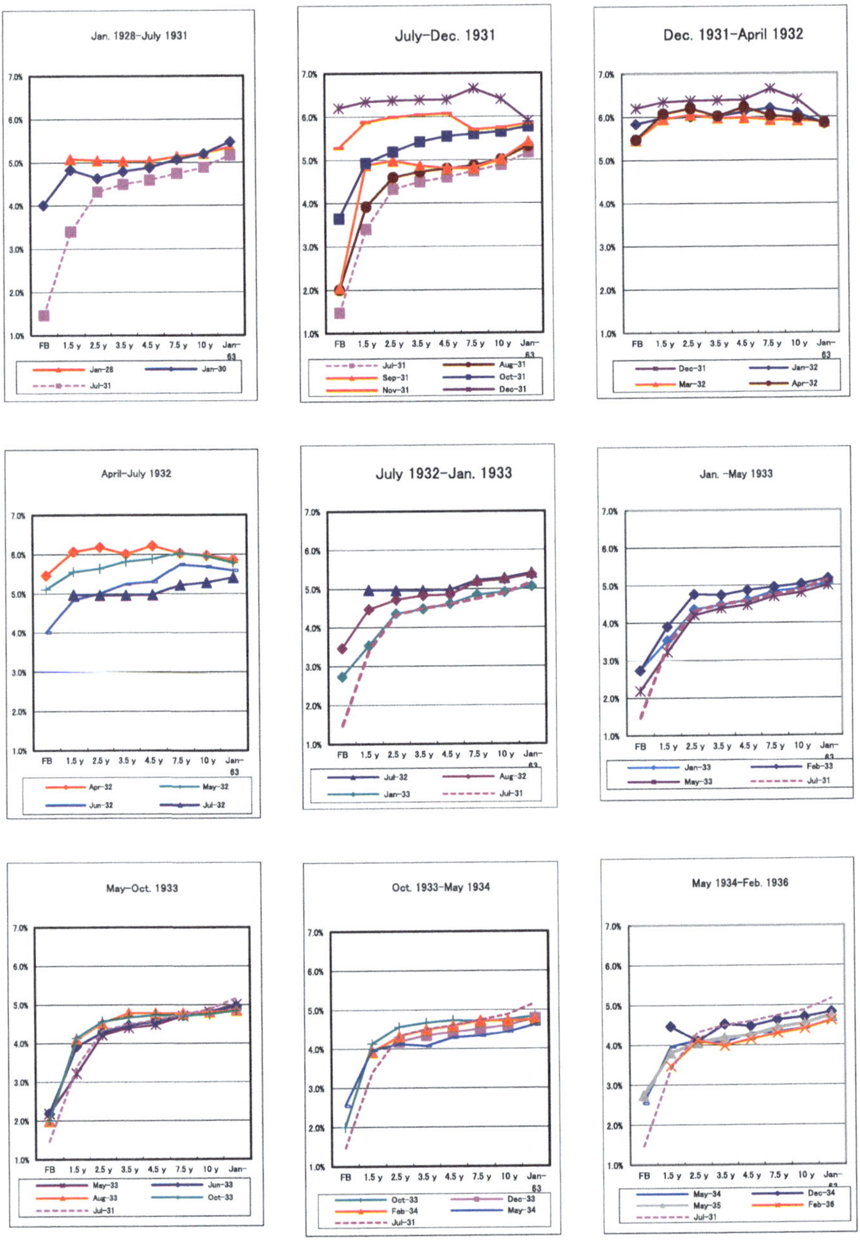

Fig. 3.9 Yield curves

The curve appeared to be upward sloping in general except from the fall of 1931 through the spring of 1932. With the lifting of the gold embargo in January 1930, the curve shifted downward until June–July 1931, when it hit bottom, indicating tranquil conditions in the financial markets. From August–September 1931 to December of that year, when it hit the peak, the curve shifted upward, with the slope being virtually flat or downturned, suggesting negative shocks due to Britain's departure from the gold standard followed by a capital flight and tight monetary policy in Japan. From December 1931, when Takahashi returned to office, to April 1932, it retained a high level. From May 1932, with an expansion in the allowance for banknote issuance without specie, the curve started shifting downward, suggesting a positive shock in the financial markets due to an accommodative monetary policy. In January 1933, the curve returned to the level of the previous low of July 1931. Subsequently, it remained more or less at or below the previous low.

3.6.3 Principal Component Analysis of JGB Yields

Principal component analysis (PCA) is a technique for "reducing the dimensionality of the dataset, increasing interpretability but at the same time minimizing information loss" (Jolliffe and Cadima 2016). With PCA, researchers may find new variables that are linear functions of those in the original dataset, which successively maximize variance and which are uncorrelated with each other.

PCA has been applied in various fields, including for the term structure of interest rates. Previous studies have found that changes in a yield curve may be explained by three factors, namely, (1) the level, (2) the slope, and (3) the curvature (Litterman and Scheinkman 1991; Bliss 1997).

Shizume (2009) employs PCA on interwar period JGB yield data to examine if the JGB market had similar properties as other credit markets and to explore the backdrop to changes in the yield curve. The formula for calculating the principal component i is:

$$X_{i,t} = \sum_{j=1}^{n} a_i^j \bullet r_{i,t}^j + \varepsilon_{i,t}^j \tag{A-2}$$

where j represents maturity, $X_{i,t}$ is the i'th principal component at period t ($i < j$), $r_{i,t}^j$ is the interest rate level of maturity j at period t, and $\epsilon_{i,t}^j$ is the residual. I use the six maturities of 1.5, 2.5, 3.5, 4.5, 7.5 and 10 year for j. PCA formulates the coefficient a_i^j to maximize the variance of $X_{i,t}$, a linear sum of interest rate fluctuations for different maturities. After determining the first principal component, $X_{1,t}$, I compute the second principal component, $X_{2,t}$, so that $X_{2,t}$ is uncorrelated with $X_{1,t}$, and then for $X_{3,t}$, and so on. Using new variables for principal components, $X_{i,t}$, movements in the term structure of interest rates can be expressed with fewer variables than in the case of the original data with different maturities. The frequency of the data is

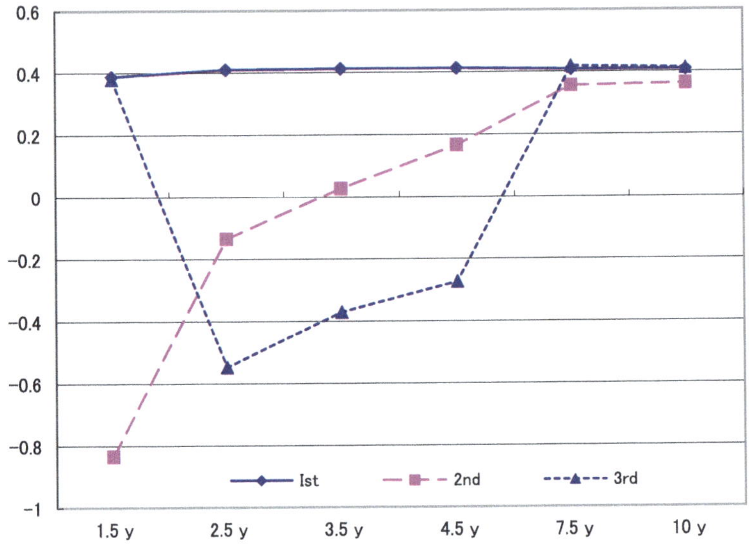

Fig. 3.10 Loadings of interest rate maturities on principal components. *Source* Shizume (2009)

monthly, and the sample period is from January 1928 to April 1936. The data in April, November, July 1929, August 1930, November and December 1933 are missing.[16]

Figure 3.10 shows the coefficients, or loadings, of interest rates on principal components. The graph of the coefficients of maturities for the first component is virtually flat at the level of around 0.4 (the average of $a_{1,1.5}$ through $a_{1,10}$ is 0.408), meaning that the first component represents the level shift of the yield curve. The graph of the coefficients of maturities for the second component is upward sloping, meaning that the second component represents the slope of the yield curve with larger values of the components lying along the flatter part of the yield curve. The graph of the coefficients of maturities for the third component is convex downward, meaning that the third component represents the curvature of the yield curve with larger values of the components lying along the more convex, downward shape of the yield curve. These results are consistent with earlier works (Litterman and Scheinkman 1991; Bliss 1997).[17]

Figure 3.11 shows developments in principal components from January 1928 to April 1936. Three components confirm the turbulent period from the fall of 1931 to the spring of 1932. The first component, which explains 95% of the interest rate fluctuation (Table 3.6), hit bottom once in June 1931, surged from August through

[16] The principal component data for the January 1928–April 1936 period is available on the Kobe University Research Institute for Economics and Business Administration (RIEB) website: https://ccss.kobe-u.ac.jp/en/research/database/.

[17] Alternatively, one may use the first difference (changes from the previous period) of the original data. I have confirmed that the result is qualitatively the same as the one using level data.

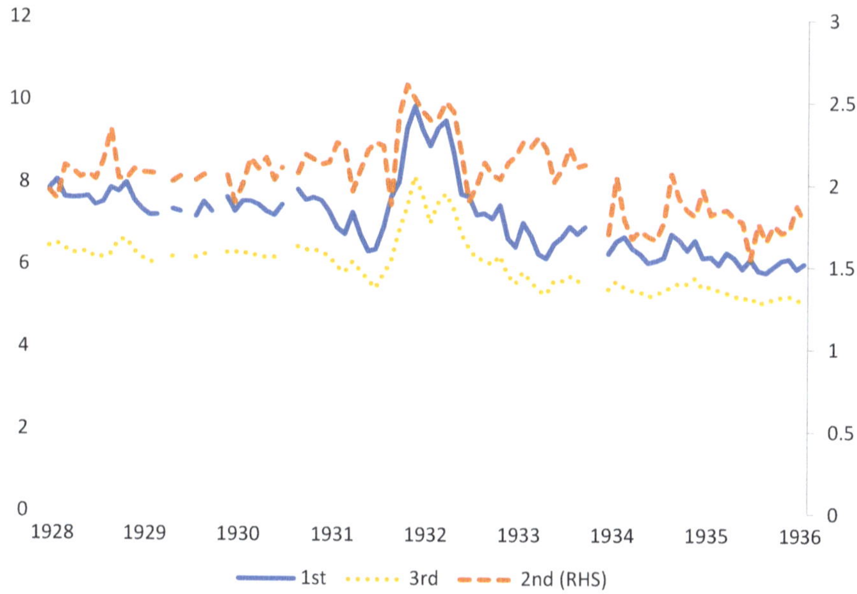

Fig. 3.11 Principal components of interest rates on government debts. *Source* Shizume (2008)

Table 3.6 Contribution of principal components to fluctuations in interest rates

	1st	2nd	3rd
Comtribution	0.954	0.031	0.009
Accumulated	0.954	0.984	0.994

*Source*Shizume (2009)

December of that year, peaking in December, stayed at a high level through April 1932, and then decreased from May of that year. In around November 1932, it returned to the level of the previous low of June 1931 and went on to hit a new low in April 1933. Subsequently, it largely stayed at or below the level of the previous low, indicating successful open market operations for achieving the policy goal of low interest rates.

3.6.4 *Views of Market Participants*

In this subsection, I provide the background to the developments in interest rates with anecdotes. Table 3.7 is a compilation of comments from the monthly TSE report. The TSE not only published statistics of prices and trade volumes but also gave a summary of the market conditions, analyzing factors based on market participants' views. The summary was published monthly in Japanese and English. According to

Table 3.7 Views published in the monthly TSE Report (U: upside news, D: downside news)

Month	On exchange rates	On monetary and fiscal policies
Jan-31	U: improvement in trade stats	U: foreign interest rate reduction, expectation of BOJ rate cut
Feb	U: improvement in trade stats	U: downward trend in interest rates
Mar		U: abundant funds, sustained low interest rates, rate cut in bank deposits
Apr	D: deterioration in trade stats	U: low interest rates in general
May		U: foreign interest rate reduction; D: saraly cut for govt. officials
June		U: sustained low interest rates
July	D: gold shipment by Yokohama Specie Bank	U: abundant funds at the beginning; D: UK interest rate hike, tight money at the end
Aug	U: stand-by credit with UK, USA and France	U: expectation of UK interesr rate reduction, interest rate cut by Deposit Bureau
Sept	D: British departure from the gold standard, deterioration in trade stats	D: deadlock of public debt policy
Oct	U: expectation of gold embargo	D: BOJ interest rate hike, US interesr rate hike
Nov	U: expectation of gold embargo	D: tight money with specie outdlows
Dec	U: gold embargo	
Jan-32	U: JPY depreciation against USD; D: fear of US gold embargo	U: expectation of stimulus policy
Feb	U: JPY depreciation against USD	U: UK interest rate reduction, US anti-austerity policy
Mar		D: tight money in local markets
Apr		U: UK interest rate reduction; D: tight money
May	U: expectation of exchange control; D: fear of US gold embargo, deteriorating trade stats	U: extention of allowance for note issuance, expectations of intererst rate reduction, UK interest rate reduction
June	U: JPY depreciation	U: BOJ interest rate cut, rescue program for rural areas, US interest rate reduction
July		U: UK interest rate reduction; D: fear of reduction in rural rescue program and/or tax increase
Aug	U: JPY depreciation	U: BOJ interest rate cut, interest rate reduction in deposits, expectation of sustained low interest rates
Sept	D: JPY appreciation	U: easy money, low interest rates
Oct	U: JPY depreciation, improvement in trade stats	U: easy money, low interest rates, expectation of BOJ interest rate cut and JGB with 4% coupon
Nov	U: JPY depreciation	U: low interest rates, reflation; D: JGB with 4.5% coupon instead of 4%
Dec	D: fear of a deadlock in exchange control issue	U: easy money, low interest rates, reflation

Source Monthly TSE reports cited in Shizume (2009)

Table 3.8 Views published in the monthly TSE Report (U: upside news, D: downside news, cont.)

Month	Other	Kō-gō 5%	1st comp.	TSE index*
Jan-31	U: bottom-out in prices of silver and commodities	5.595	7.320	0.6
Feb	U: stable prices of silver and commodities, surge in raw cotton price	5.506	6.937	5.5
Mar.	U: surge in raw cotton price, agreements in sugar production and navigation companies	5.390	6.777	6.3
Apr.	D: drop in commodity prices and US stocks, uncertain political situation	5.385	7.306	−1.5
May	D: drop in commodity prices, deteriaration in US economy, uncertain political situation	5.314	6.759	−2.1
June	U: surge in US stocks, silver and commodity prices by Hoover Moratoriun	5.201	6.367	4.2
July	U: UK-France agreement on reparation; D: drop in US stocks and commodity prices, German financial crisis	5.176	6.415	7.5
Aug.	U: UK national coallition; D: fear of deteriorating business condition	5.321	6.925	−5.6
Sept	D: Manchuria Incident, drop in US stocks and domestic/foreign commodity prices	5.427	7.689	−3.0
Oct.	D: deterioration in US economy, expansion of Manchuria Incident into foreign relations	5.774	8.049	−13.8
Nov.	U: expectation of national coallition, favorable atomosphere in the League of Nations, victory in North Manchuria; D: drop in US stocks and cotton	5.848	9.347	3.2
Dec.	U: Seiyūkai government; D: fear of deteriorating US economy	5.909	9.894	12.4
Jan-32	U: expectation of victory of ruling party in election; D: Shanghai Incident, fear of deteriorating foreign relations	5.849	9.332	23.6
Feb	D: expansion of Shanghai Incident, deteriorating foreign relations in the League of Nations	5.900	8.930	2.1
Mar.	D: disappointment in economic policy, unfavorable in the League of Nations, fear of sanctions by US, Deteriorating US economy, drops in domestic/foreign commodity prices	5.892	9.362	-3.4
Apr.	D: deteriorating US economy, drop in domestic commodity prices, deteriarating condition in Shanghai	5.865	9.547	-7.9
May	D: May 15 Incident, drop in domestic commodity prices	5.793	8.780	0.5
June	U: surge in commodity prices	5.593	7.758	−6.2
July	D: Lytton Commission report, China-Japan confrontation, fear of Indian tariff hike	5.412	7.703	3.4

(continued)

Table 3.8 (continued)

Month	Other	Kō-gō 5%	1st comp.	TSE index*
Aug.	U: surge in US stocks, surge in domestic commodity price by JPY depreciation; D: fear of the unfavorable League of Nations, uncertainty in political situation	5.373	7.252	2.3
Sept	U: recognition of Manchukuo, improvement in foreign relations; D: Drops in US stocks and domestic/international commodity prices	5.219	7.285	7.4
Oct.	U: surge in domestic commodity prices, expectation of imprivement in business condition; D: unfavorable Lytton Commission report	5.175	7.162	0.6
Nov.	U: expectation of improvement in business condition, Roosevelt for US presitdent; D: the unfavorable League of Nations	5.087	7.488	14.5
Dec.	D: the unfavorable League of Nations	5.065	6.689	20.3

* Percent change from the previous month

the report, market participants were well informed of international events as well as domestic economic and political developments.

The TSE report highlighted the backdrop to interest rate movements. From fall to winter of 1931, the British departure from the gold standard and the Manchurian Incident triggered a capital outflow. This was coupled with a deterioration of the US economy. Starting October 1931, well ahead of actual gold embargo in December that year, market participants began anticipating the embargo. After the actual gold embargo in December 1931, until April 1932, market participants maintained a cautious stance, facing deteriorating international relations due to the expansion of military operations in Manchuria and Shanghai and the US economic depression. In May 1932, notwithstanding the assassination of Prime Minister Inukai in the May 15 Incident, the expansion of the allowance for banknote issuance prompted stronger expectations of monetary easing. From June 1932, the government's policy actions successfully reversed the perceptions of market participants despite a deterioration in international relations.

References

Aoki, Shiichi. 1932. *Futsū ginkō kashidashi gyōmu (Ordinary bank's lending business)*. Tokyo: Shibun Shoin.

Bank of Japan. Various issues. *Kin'yū shiryō yōroku* (Abstract of financial materials). Tokyo: Bank of Japan.

Bank of Japan. 1956. *Nihon kin'yūshi shiryō: Meiji-Taishō hen* (Materials on Japanese financial history: the Meiji-Taishō period), 18. Tokyo: Bank of Japan.

Bank of Japan. 1973. *Nihon kin'yūshi shiryō: Shōwa hen* (Materials on Japanese financial history: the Shōwa period), 34. Tokyo: Bank of Japan.

Bank of Japan. 1984. *Nippon ginkō hyakunen shi* (The first hundred years of the Bank of Japan), 4. Tokyo: Bank of Japan.

Bliss, Robert R. 1997. Movements in the term structure of interest rates. *Federal Reserve Bank of Atlanta Economic Review* Fourth Quarter: 16-33.

Eichengreen, Barry. 1992. *Golden fetters: the gold standard and the Great Depression: 1919–1939*. New York: Oxford University Press.

Fujino, Shōzaburō, and Jūrō Teranishi. 2000. *Nihon kin'yū no sūryō bunseki* (A quantitative analysis of Japanese finance). Tokyo: Tōyō Keizai Shinpōsha.

Fukai, Eigo. 1938. *Kinhon'isei ridatsugo no tsūka seisaku* (Monetary policy after the departure from the gold standard). Tokyo: Chikura Shobō.

Fukai, Eigo. 1941. *Kaiko nanajuūnen* (Reflections on the past seventy years). Tokyo: Iwanami Shoten.

Gotō, Shin'ichi. 1970. *Nihon no kin'yū tōkei* (Financial statistics of Japan). Tokyo: Tōyō Keizai Shinpōsha.

Hirayama, Ken'ichi. 2019. *Senzen senji ki no kin'yū shijō* (Financial markets in Japan in the pre-war and the wartime periods). Tokyo: Nikkei Shinbun Shuppan Sha.

Ide, Eisaku. 2006. *Takahashi zaisei no kenkyū* (A thesis on Takahashi Economic Policy). Tokyo: Yūhikaku.

Inoue, Toshikazu. 2011. *Senzen nihon no gurōbarizumu* (Globalism in the pre-war Japan). Tokyo: Shinchō Sensho.

Ishibashi, Tanzan. 1929. *Kin-kaikin no eikyō to taisaku: shin-heika kin-kaikin no teishō* (Effects of the lifting of gold embargo: a proposal for the lifting of gold embargo with a new parity). Tokyo: Tōyō Keizai Shinpōsha.

Jolliffe, Ian T., and Jorge Cadima. 2016. Principal component analysis: a review and recent developments. Philosophical Transactions of the Royal Society A, 374.

Kawakami, K. K. Britain's trade War with Japan. *Foreign Affairs* 12(3), 483–494.

Keynes, John Maynard. 1925. The economic consequences of Mr. Churchill. *The Nation and Athenaeum*, 2 May 1925. Reprinted in *The collected writing of John Maynard Keynes*, Part 1, London: Royal Economic Society, 1978.

Keynes, John Maynard, and Hubert Douglas Henderson. 1929. Can Lloyd George do it? An examination of the Liberal pledge. *The Nation and Athenaeum*. May 1, 1929. London: 2-44.

Litterman, Robert, and Jose Scheinkman. 1991. Common factors affecting bond returns. *Journal of Fixed Income* 1: 54–61.

Ministry of Finance. Various issues. *Ōkurashō nenpō* (Yearbook of the Ministry of Finance). Tokyo: Ministry of Finance.

Ministry of Finance. Various issues. *Kin'yū jikō sankō sho* (Reference book of financial matters). Tokyo: The Ministry of Finance.

Ministry of Finance. 1936. *Meiji Taishō zeisei shi* (Financial history of the Meiji Taishō periods), 11. Tokyo: Zaisei Keizai Gakkai.

Ministry of Finance. 1955. *Shōwa zaisei shi* (Financial history of the Shōwa period), 4. Tokyo: Tōyō Keizai Shinpōsha.

Ministry of Finance. 1965. *Shōwa zaisei shi* (Financial history of the Shōwa period), 1. Tokyo: Tōyō Keizai Shinpōsha.

Obstfeld, Maurice, Jay C. Shambaugh, and Alan M. Taylor. 2004. Monetary sovereignty, exchange rates, and capital controls: the trilemma in the interwar period. *IMF Staff Paper*, 51, Special Issue, International Monetary Fund.

Shizume, Masato. 2008. Ryō taisen kanki Nihon no chōki kinri shihyō: Tokyo kabushiki torihikijo ni okeru jōjō kokusai no kakaku dēta o mochiita suikei (Indexes of long-term interest rates in Japan during the interwar period: estimates using price data of the listed government bonds at the Tokyo Stock Exchange). *RIEB Discussion Paper* J98. www.rieb.kobe-u.ac.jp/academic/ra/dp/Japanese/dpJ98.pdf (accessed on February 21, 2021).

Shizume, Masato. 2009. *Sekai kyōkō to keizai seisaku: kaihō shōkoku Nihon no keiken to gendai* (The world depression and economic policy: lessons from Japan as a small open economy). Tokyo: Nikkei Shinbun Shuppan Sha.

Shizume, Masato. 2018. Financial crises and the central bank: lessons from Japan during the 1920s. Rockoff, Hugh, and Isao Suto eds. *Coping with financial crises: some lessons from financial history*, Singapore: Springer Nature: 131-148.

Takeda, Masaru. 2012. 1920 nendai ni okeru gensai kikin to kokusai kakaku (Sinking fund and JGB prices in the 1920s). *RIPESS Working Paper* 43, 56–76.

Chapter 4
Sustainability of Public Debt Under Stress

While Takahashi's policy package brought the Japanese economy out of the Great Depression, crises in the international and domestic political scenes continued. Takahashi negotiated with the military ministers to alleviate the burden on public finances of the operation on mainland China and the buildup of arms. I revisit his struggle with pressures resulting from military expansionism from the perspective of fiscal and public debt policy governance in the long term.

4.1 Sustainability of Public Debt in the Long Run

We need to explore the modern political history of Japan from a more long-term perspective to understand the sustainability of the country's public debt. In this chapter, I will discuss the governance of public finance focusing on the work of the Japanese government as a modern fiscal state.[1]

After a forced opening of treaty ports as part of the gunboat diplomacy of Commodore Matthew Perry of the United States in the 1850s, Japan experienced years of turbulence in the form of civil wars and uprisings, including the 1868 Meiji Restoration and subsequent civil wars. To keep its independence, the new Meiji Government set itself the dual goal of establishing a "rich country, (with a) strong military" (*fukoku kyōhei*).

In the 1870s through the early 1880s, the Japanese government successfully implemented drastic fiscal reforms. It eliminated feudal stipend payments to samurai (*chitsuroku shobun*), introduced a unified land tax system (*chiso kaisei*), and consolidated the debts inherited from the Tokugawa Shogunate and domain governments. By the late 1880s, the modern fiscal state had emerged in Japan (He 2013: 128). At the same time, it promoted industry by mobilizing capital and labor, introducing advanced

[1] For the establishment of a modern fiscal state, see He (2013: 105–130).

M. Shizume, *The Japanese Economy During the Great Depression*,
Studies in Economic History,
https://doi.org/10.1007/978-981-13-7357-2_4

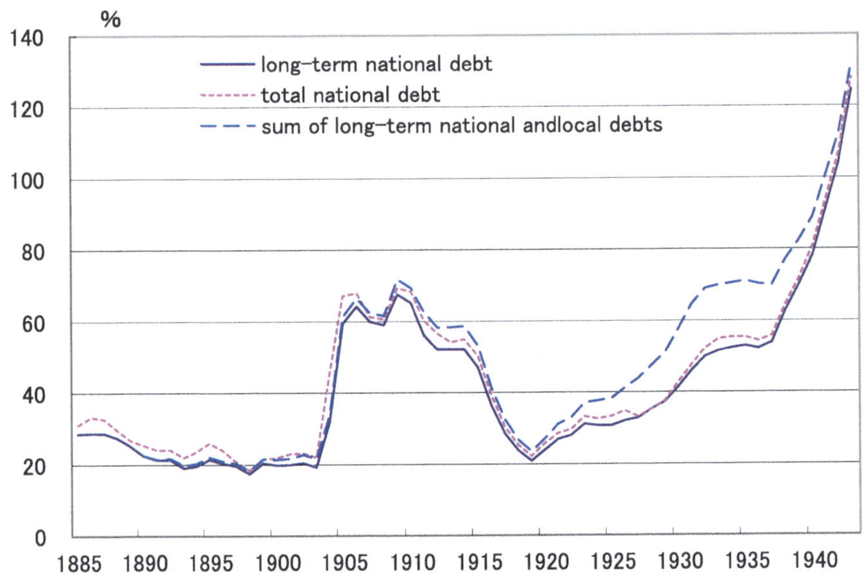

Fig. 4.1 Public debt, 1885–1943 (as % of GNP). *Source* MOF (1955, various issues), Ohkawa et al. (1974), Shizume (2011)

technologies and socio-economic systems from the West, and integrating them with existing domestic technologies and systems (*shokusan kōgyō*).

Although, in principle, the two goals of "rich country" and "strong military" were pursued in tandem, in practice they were sometimes in conflict (Banno 2014; Shizume 2018). As early as 1873, a faction of veterans insisted on sending troops to Korea to conduct gunboat diplomacy as the Western powers had done with Japan less than two decades previously. Under the aegis of China, Korea refused to open its ports. Ōkubo Toshimichi, an influential statesman at the time, rejected the proposal of exercising military might on Korea because Japan lacked the fiscal base for taking on the risk of war with China. Instead, he initiated full-fledged programs for fiscal reform and industrial growth.

After establishing a modern fiscal state within the first two decades of the Meiji Era (1868–1911), Japan raised its ambitions from merely preserving its independence to building an empire in east Asia. It won colonies following the First Sino-Japanese War (1894–1895) and Russo-Japanese War (1904–1905). The burden of maintaining and expanding its imperial sphere then raised the question of how to allocate domestic resources and how to finance nation-building.[2]

Figure 4.1 shows public debt for the fiscal years 1885–1943 (Shizume 2011: 1115). The average long-term national debt over the sample period was 42% of the gross national product (GNP). It was stable at under 30% until the outbreak of the

[2] Jones and Ericson (2007) provide a concise and comprehensive guide to the socio-economic and political history of Japan from the late nineteenth to the early twentieth century.

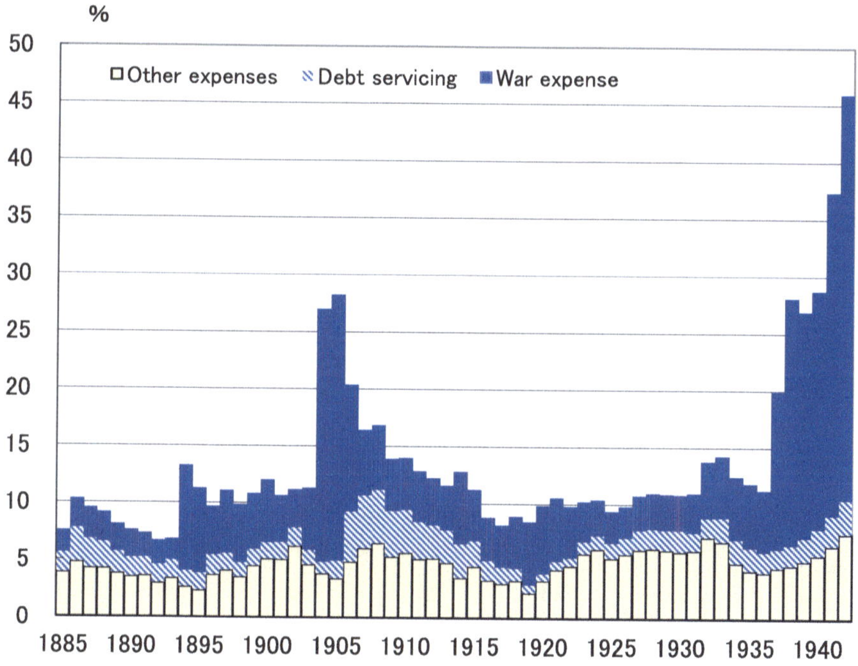

Fig. 4.2 Fiscal expenditure, 1885–1942 (as % of GNP). *Source* MOF (1955), Ohkawa and Shinohara (1979), Shizume (2009)

Russo-Japanese War, then soared during the war, up to 65% at the end of 1906. It remained at around 60% until the outbreak of WWI, before falling during the war to 21% at the end of 1919. It crept up during the 1920s to 42%, the average level of the whole sample period, at the end of 1930, and then jumped during the first half of Takahashi's term in 1931–1936, and stayed at the 50–60% level for the rest of his term. It skyrocketed after his assassination in 1936.

Figure 4.2 shows the burden of government expenditure on the Japanese national economy. Before the First Sino-Japanese War in 1894–1895, fiscal expenditure was from seven to ten percent of GNP. It increased to 13% in 1894 and then remained at around ten percent until the outbreak of the Russo-Japanese War in 1904. The Russo-Japanese War imposed a heavy burden on the national economy via direct war spending during the war and debt servicing afterwards.

Shizume (2011) employs Bohn's method to test the sustainability of the Japanese public debt with a new dataset of primary balance and government debt from 1885 to 1940 and finds that the sustainability of public debt was lost in the early 1930s.

Bohn's method tests the relationship between public debt and the primary fiscal balance, to be interpreted as a reaction function of the government's debt-to-GNP ratio by means of the operation of fiscal balance. The basic notion is that, if a government improves its primary balance when it sees the public debt/output ratio increasing, then its public debt will remain sustainable. In other words, public debt

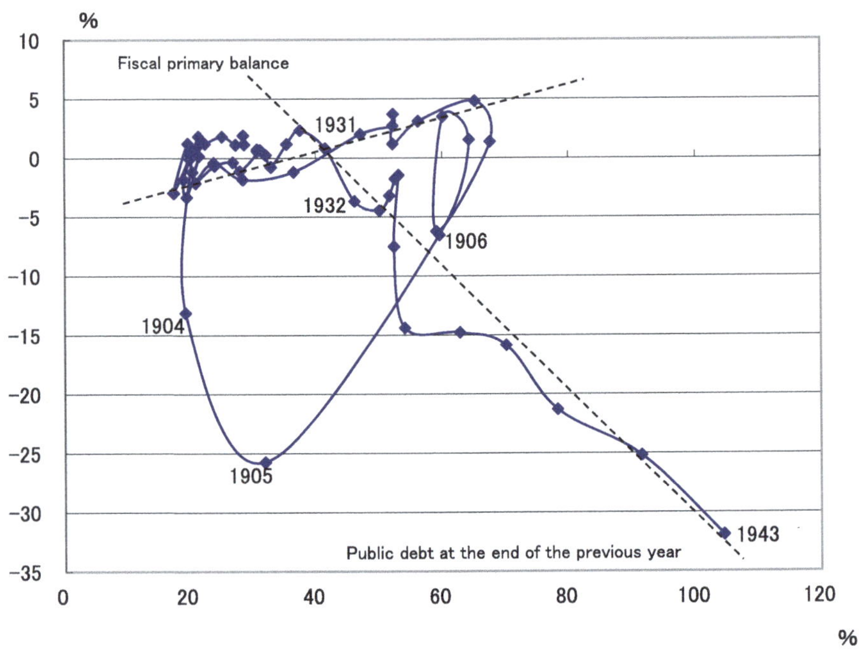

Fig. 4.3. Fiscal balance and public debt (as % of GNP). *Source* MOF (1936,1954), Ohkawa et al. (1974,1979), Shizume (2011)

is sustainable so long as the government employ an austerity policy when it sees the fiscal condition deteriorating.

To visualize the condition, Shizume draws a figure following Doi and Nakazato (2004) with the primary fiscal balance on the vertical axis and the public debt on the horizontal axis, both expressed as a percentage of GNP (Fig. 4.3). If the two variables maintain a positive correlation (an upward sloping graph), public debt is sustainable; otherwise, it is unsustainable. From the graph, it is clear that the two variables maintained a positive correlation until 1931, except around the time of the Russo-Japanese War (1904–1905), but acquired a negative correlation after this point. This structural change is confirmed by a structural break test.[3]

The author's interpretation of the above result is that, for some reason, the Japanese government lost fiscal discipline around the early 1930s. It should be noted that the statistical relationship only indicates a change in correlation between public debt and primary fiscal balance, while saying nothing about the reason for the change or the background to the loss of sustainability of public debt. These will have to be explored through historical accounts.

[3] The full sample of the fiscal balances and the public debt data for the 1885–1943 period is available on the Kobe University Research Institute for Economics and Business Administration (RIEB) website: http://ccss.kobe-u.ac.jp/en/research/database/.

4.2 Governance of Public Finance in Japan Under the Meiji Constitution

To inquire into the historical account of the loss of fiscal discipline, we should first review the modern political history of Japan. Table 4.1 shows the chronology of political events in modern Japan. Recent studies explore the long process of the expansion of political participation, starting from the closing days of the Tokugawa Shogunate and through the carefully designed Meiji Constitution of 1889. The constitution divided political power between political and economic leaders, mainly from the lower samurai class from the Satsuma and Chōshū domains, and the new class of commoners consisting of peasants and merchants who paid taxes (Mitani 1997, 2013, 2017). In dealing with the popular rights movement during the 1870s and 1880s, the designers of the constitution established a system of checks and balances governing the administrative and legislative branches in favor of the former. The designers used the Prussian constitution as the model, intending to control the power of taxpayers while appeasing them. They also gave power to some of the players in the administrative branch under the supreme emperor (Banno 1992,2014).

On the eve of Japan's confrontation with the Western powers and its own modernization, the central government of Japan, the Tokugawa Shogunate (1603–1867), comprised a small number of selected lords (*daimyo*) and direct retainers of the shogun (*hatamoto*), while the domains were independently governed by the individual lords. When the shogunate was forced to open treaty ports in the late 1850s, it began inviting powerful lords and their retainers to the national political arena to help overcome the crisis (Mitani 1997, 2013, 2017; Banno 2014).

During the first two decades after the Meiji Restoration (1868), the new Meiji Government, having overthrown the shogunate, further expanded political participation among the samurai and commoners. This was done because the government needed to mobilize financial and human capital toward nation-building, and the people asked for political participation in return for their contributions. The government pursued nation-building under the slogans of "rich county, strong military" (*fukoku kyōhei*) and "fairness and public opinion" (*kōgi yoron*). In 1874, eight samurai, mainly from Kochi Prefecture (formerly the Tosa Province), submitted a Petition to Establish a Popularly Elected Assembly to the government, arguing that "[t]hose people having the duty to pay tax to the government also have the right to support or reject what the government is doing." Given that, in those days, the main national tax was land tax paid by farmers, the statement implied the political participation of farmers in national politics through a parliamentary system. In response, the government issued an Imperial Proclamation in 1875 to "establish gradually a form of constitutional government structure." However, in the 1870s, opposition to the government was often expressed in the form of violent actions such as civil wars, riots, and attacks on government institutions and prominent figures, rather than through open debate and political negotiation (Banno 2014: 53–82; Mitani 2017: 309–316).

Table 4.1 Chronology of political events in Japan, 1850–1945

Year	Event
1853	Commodore Perry sails into Uraga Bay
1854	Japan-US Treaty of Peace and Amity; similar treaties with Great Britain and Russia
1858	Japan-US Treaty of Amity and Commerce
1859	Yokohama, Hakodate and Nagasaki opened as treaty ports
1868	Proclamation of Imperial Restoration
1868–1869	Boshin War
1871	New Currency Act; abolition of domains, introduction of prefectures
1873	Proclamation of conscription ordinance; ordinance on land tax; split over question of invading Korea
1874	Petition to establish a popularly elected assembly
1875	Imperial proclamation on establishment of a constitutional system
1876	Measures to abolish stipend payments for former samurai
1877	Land tax reduction (from 3 to 2.5%); Satsuma Rebellion
1881	Ōkuma Shigenobu and Inoue Kowashi submit proposals for constitution; Ōkuma ousted
1889	Promulgation of the Great Japan Imperial Constitution
1890	First general election, imperial diet (parliament) opened
1894–1895	First Sino-Japanese war
1899	Treaty revision accomplished (legal rights restored)
1900	Electoral law revision (expansion of suffrage); convention that army and navy ministers must be serving officers
1902	Anglo-Japanese Alliance
1904–1905	Russo-Japanese War
1910	Incorporation of Korea into Japan
1911	Restoration of tariff autonomy; Chinese revolution of 1911
1912–1913	First constitutional protection movement
1913	Removal of requirement for service ministers to be serving ministers
1915	Twenty-one demands to China
1924	Second constitutional protection movement
1925	Male Universal Suffrage Act
1931	Mukden incident; departure from the gold standard
1932	May 15th incident (Inukai Tsuyoshi assassinated)
1936	February 26th incident (Saitō Makoto and Takahashi Korekiyo assassinated); Requirement for service ministers to be serving ministers resumed
1937	Marco Polo Bridge incident (Second Sino-Japanese War breaks out)
1941	Attack on Pearl Harbor

(continued)

Table 4.1 (continued)

Year	Event
1945	Potsdam proclamation (unconditional surrender)

Source Banno 2014

After the Satsuma Rebellion of 1877, the last civil war in Japan, political decisions came to be made through discussion and negotiation rather than the use of military power. In 1881, when the government promised to establish a constitution, it rejected the British "cabinet within parliament" system proposed by former Finance Minister Ōkuma Shigenobu and, instead, adopted the Prussian system of "constitutional monarchy" proposed by Inoue Kowashi, a bureaucrat who had studied the German and French legal systems. In 1881, ousted from the government due to a dispute over the constitution, Ōkuma left and established Japan's first political party, the Rikken Kaishintō (Constitutional Progressive Party), the following year (Banno 2014: 83–120).

The Great Japan Imperial Constitution was promulgated in 1889 based on Inoue's proposal, and gave the emperor and the executive branch more powerful rights than the parliament. The House of Peers (kizokuin, the upper house) consisted of nobles and former bureaucrats who were expected to vote for the executive. Even so, the House of Representatives (shūgiin, the lower house) could exercise the veto on proposals related to fiscal spending, including military expenses, and/or taxation by the administrative branch on behalf of the electorate (Banno 2014: 108–116). Commoners acquired the right to express their opinions through public debate. At the same time, the elder statesmen (*genrō*), who were trusted by the emperor as informal advisors to recommend a candidate for prime minister without any description in the constitution, played a reconciliatory role behind the scenes (Mosk 2007: 94–95).

When Ōkuma was ousted from the government in 1881, Matsukata Masayoshi became the finance minister and went on to oversee the national public finance for almost two decades. Matsukata is famous for a fiscal austerity program that he is believed to have initiated at the start of his tenure as finance minister, but recent studies revisit his achievements and find his approach incremental rather than hardline, with monetary stability prioritized as a prerequisite for the development of a modern economy and society. Matsutaka established the BOJ in 1882. He made the BOJ issue notes convertible to silver in 1885 and made existing government notes convertible to silver in 1886, thereby introducing a silver standard. If Inoue's proposal established the legal foundations of Japan's modern nation-building, Matsukata's financial reforms laid the groundwork for the country's economic growth and development as a modern nation (Banno 2014: 92–100; Ericson 2019: 135–138).

Right from the time the constitution and the foundations of modern public finance were established in the 1880s, Japan's public finance faced several challenges through the 1940s. Most of these challenges were owing to the country's military expansion in an effort to build an empire in east Asia and the resulting conflict between having a "rich country" versus a "strong military." The government wanted to extend the front from the Korean peninsula, where it was during the First Sino-Japanese War (1894–1895), to the Chinese mainland during and after the Russo-Japanese War (1904–1905). Taxpayers, mainly consisting of landowners, demanded the government ease tax burdens or, at least, avoid tax increases through the House of Representatives. Compromises were made between leaders on the administrative and political sides (Matsusaka 2007; Banno 2014: 116–143).

The expansion of political participation further complicated the resolution of the conflict. In the early days of the parliament, the two poles of debate were the executive led by veterans of the Restoration mainly from Satsuma and Chōshū, and the opposition parties in the House of Representatives elected by landowners who paid land taxes. The main agenda was whether to accelerate military buildup to prepare for war in Asia or to give taxpayers, who bore the burden of the military buildup, a break. After the Seiyūkai was established in 1900 as the conservative party representing local taxpayers' interests, it achieved a reconciliation between the executive and legislative branches by proposing a developmental state model associated with pork-barrel politics (Banno 1992,2014).

Industrialization and economic development resulted in the multipolarization of domestic politics. At the same time, demands for further political participation in the form of universal male suffrage spread nationwide. The tax payment criteria for suffrage was lowered from a minimum annual tax payment of 15 yen in 1889 to three yen in 1919 (Table 4.2, left). A two-party system emerged during the 1910s and 1920s consisting of the conservative Seiyūkai and the liberal Kenseikai (later Minseitō, Large 2007: 163–165). Swings in the number of seats between the two parties reflected the dynamism of Japanese politics in 1920s and the early 1930s. This was the heyday of democracy in prewar Japan, and the two parties formed and maintained the cabinet based on their electoral support.

4.3 Sustainability of Public Debt and the Gold Standard

As policymakers for a small, open economy, Japan's leaders monitored conditions in the international financial markets and were concerned about the country's reputation among international investors (Suzuki 1994, Bytheway 2014).

Initially, the Meiji Government adopted a cautious stance toward borrowing from foreign lenders for reasons of national security, namely, to avoid the risk of colonization in case of a default on the debt (Mitchener et al. 2010a; Mitchener and Weidenmier 2010b). However, once it realized that it was no longer under threat of being colonized, it became more accepting of external financing to obtain the extra funds required for its empire-building efforts. At around the turn of the century, Japan came to be recognized as a legally equal partner of the Western powers, and the government succeeded in revising its unequal treaties with them (Mitchener et al. 2010a; Shizume 2018). The government moved to adopt the gold standard in 1897 as a prerequisite for massive fundraising in the international financial markets. Indeed,

Table 4.2 Japan's electoral system and general election results, 1889–1942

	Electorate		General election (House of representatives)								
Legislation	Tax payment	Number					Number of seats by party				
Year	criteria	(Thousands)		Year	Month	Day	Liberal/Seiyūkai	Progressive/Kenseikai/Minseitō	Other	Vacant	Total
1889	15 yen+	450	1	1890	July	1	130	40	130	4	300
			2	1892	Feb	15	94	38	168	0	300
			3	1894	Mar	1	119	48	133	0	300
			4	1894	Sept	1	106	45	149	0	300
			5	1898	Mar	15	98	91	111	0	300
			6	1898	Aug	10	119	123	58	0	300
1900	10 yen+	1000	7	1902	Aug	10	191	93	92	0	376
			8	1903	Mar	1	174	85	117	1	376
			9	1904	Mar	1	130	90	159	1	379
			10	1908	May	15	193	65	121	0	379
			11	1912	May	15	212	87	82	0	381
			12	1915	Mar	25	206	91	84	1	381
			13	1917	April	20	160	119	102	0	381
1919	3 yen+	3000	14	1920	May	10	282	108	73	1	463
			15	1924	May	10	101	154	209	0	464
1925	None	12,400	16	1928	Feb	20	221	214	31	2	466
			17	1930	Feb	20	172	269	25	2	466
			18	1932	Feb	20	303	144	19	0	466
1934	None	14,000	19	1936	Feb	20	170	204	92	0	466

(continued)

Table 4.2 (continued)

Legislation	Electorate		General election (House of representatives)								
	Tax payment	Number					Number of seats by party				
Year	criteria	(Thousands)		Year	Month	Day	Liberal/Seiyūkai	Progressive/Kenseikai/Minseitō	Other	Vacant	Total
			20	1937	April	30	175	180	111	0	466
			21	1942	April	30	0	0	466	0	466

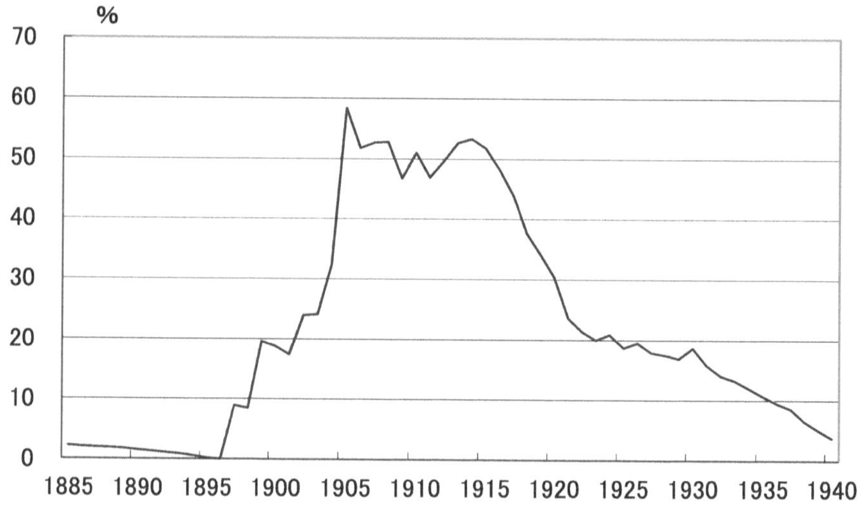

Fig. 4.4 Public debt held by overseas agents. *Source* Fujino and Teranishi (2000)

the Japanese side of the Russo-Japanese War was funded by European and American money, with Takahashi playing a central role in fundraising (Smethurst 2007: 141–187). When the war ended, overseas investors held over half of Japan's national debt (Fig. 4.4) and, unless Japanese taxpayers repaid this external debt, international investors would impose a high risk premium on JGBs. Takahashi warned the Tokyo government of the need for a prudent fiscal policy in a cable to Matsuo Shigeyoshi, the BOJ governor, as he negotiated on the condition of bond issuance with bankers in London in September 1905 immediately after the ceasefire[4]:

> The government must insure that imports are limited to productive goods and capital.... It must open the way to find capital for productive enterprise.... Each minister, and especially the army and navy minister, must consider what facilities are most important to him, and whether or not the nation's wealth is adequate to support them. Tell this to all of the ministers. Each individual allocation must be decided on the basis of a unified national fiscal policy. If we act hastily beyond our national power and do not think out and plan what we do, we shall fall into the tragedy of national bankruptcy...

At the time of the Russo-Japanese War, the government unanimously supported public debt sustainability because, for continuing the war, it was crucial to be credible to international investors. As the war approached its conclusion, the army and navy began to recognize their limited capacity for war, realizing that they would not be able to continue fighting if the JGB lost credibility in the international financial markets. They, therefore, cooperated with the other members of the executive branch.

Following the introduction of the gold standard in 1897, Japan maintained gold convertibility for 20 years, but suspended it in 1917 following the United States. In

[4] Takahashi's cable to Governor Matsuo, September 6, 1905, Matsuo Shigeyoshi papers, BOJ Archives, No. 67144, quoted in Smethurst (2007: 183).

the years after the Russo-Japanese War, when international investors were worried about the capacity and political will of the Japanese government to repay the debt, the government adopted austerity measures to prove its capacity and will to repay (Kamiyama 1995; Shizume 2011). Even during the suspension of the gold standard between 1917 and 1929, the government acted as though on a shadow gold standard (Metzler 2006). This is reminiscent of a notion proposed by Bordo and Rockoff (1996) of "the gold standard as a good housekeeping seal of approval."

In 1920, Takahashi went on to propose the abolition of the army's General Staff Office, as finance minister in the Hara Takashi Cabinet, the first cabinet to be made up entirely of a political party, the Seiyūkai. Takahashi argued that "[the General Staff Office] is placed outside the sphere of national politics and occupies a place of independence and lack of constraint, though not only in military matters but also in foreign policy…. It should rather be abolished, Army administration should be unified, and we should expect a renewal of our foreign policy."[5]

Perhaps the most radical proposal came from Ishibashi Tanzan, an economist and the chief editor of *Tōyō Keizai Shinpō*, an economics magazine. In a series of editorial articles on the Washington Naval Disarmament Conference in 1921, he proposed withdrawing from overseas territories, including Manchuria and the Korean peninsula, to reduce military spending. He argued that the cost of maintaining territories such as Korea, Taiwan, and Manchuria, including stationed troops and investment in their development, would exceed benefits from the territories; that the time had come for empires to give independence to their colonies, and to make it outdated to obtain new colonies; and that militaristic aggression would create antagonism with neighboring countries, while the relinquishment of external territories would create a favorable relationships with major trading partners, including the United States and China (Ishibashi 1921a, b, c, d).

The proposals of Takahashi and Ishibashi echoed concerns about embedded expansionism within the military and were aimed at controlling military spending (Kyō 1992: 401). However, these proposals were not embraced until after the end of World War II.

As part of the fiscal 1920 budget negotiations as finance minister of the Hara Cabinet, Takahashi discussed military spending with the army and navy ministers prior to the regular budgetary process. Takahashi wanted to cut fiscal expenditure including military spending, and Army Minister Tanaka Giichi agreed to cooperate by cutting the army budget. This episode fostered trust between Takahashi and Tanaka and, four years later, Takahashi recommended Tanaka to succeed him as head of the Seiyūkai (Takahashi 1936a: 50–52). Notwithstanding this, Takahashi circulated a document among his fellow politicians containing a proposal to abolish the Army General Staff Office with the intention of eliminating the institutional source of excess spending that often demanded its own budget be increased irrespective of national budget constraints (Smethurst 2007: 220).

---

[5] *Ogawa Heikichi kankei monjo* (Materials relating to Ogawa Heikichi), vol. 2: 140–141, quoted in Banno (2014): 170.

Economic growth during the World War I boom and subsequent disarmament lessened the burden of military expenditure on the national economy at least temporarily. Economic growth reduced the burden by expanding the denominator, while disarmament did so by shrinking the numerator. The government allocated its surplus resources for such civilian uses as restoration and reconstruction after the Great Kanto Earthquake in 1923 and financial stabilization following the panic of 1927.

International disarmament also contributed to alleviating the burden of military expenditure. Japan participated in the Washington Naval Disarmament Conference in 1921–1922 and Takahashi concluded the naval treaty as prime minister after the assassination of Hara. Japan ratified the 1928 Kellogg–Briand Pact, officially known as the General Treaty for Renunciation of War as an Instrument of National Policy (Smethurst 2007: 226–227).

4.4 Loss of Public Debt Sustainability in the Early 1930s

Shizume (2011) attributes the loss of public debt sustainability to two reasons: (1) an effective veto by the military in the budgeting process, and (2) the weakening governance mechanism of the international financial markets. The former was domestic and of an institutional origin, and the latter was external and newly incurred due to the departure of Britain from the gold standard. I will explore the background to the loss of sustainability in greater detail by looking into historical accounts of the political economy in prewar Japan.

When nationwide male universal suffrage was introduced in 1925, the emerging two-party parliamentary cabinet system was expected to absorb and coordinate the diverse interests of various groups, including the military, taxpayers (comprising landowners, merchants, and the new middle class of intellectual workers, such as government officials and business elites), as well as the part of the electorate that did not pay income tax. However, political parties proved to be incapable of coordinating various interests and reconciling conflicts. They tended to fight with each other rather than cooperate for the sake of democracy, which eroded their support from the general public. People gradually began to distrust political parties for their corrupt liaisons with financial cliques (*zaibatsu*) and to lean either toward the military, which was seen as devoting itself to national security, or toward radical socialist movements, which attracted those with progressive ideas who had once supported a parliamentary liberal democracy. The latter would be harshly suppressed in the 1930s (Inoue 2012).

Further, a rise in terrorism and coup attempts depleted the political capital of party politicians by literally killing off prominent figures and silencing survivors. Table 4.3 shows the prevalence of political assassinations in the 1930s, with an unprecedented number of victims.

Britain's departure from the gold standard and the Mukden Incident, both in September 1931, marked a turn in the tide of Japanese public finance governance.

First, Britain's departure from the gold standard on September 21, 1931, effectively cut off Japan's public finance from the international financial markets. The

Table 4.3 Assassinations of prominent figures (1868–1936)

Name of the victim	Year	Occupation/career
Yokoi Shōnan	1869	Educator
Ōmura Masujirō	1869	Politician
Hirosawa Saneomi	1871	Politician
Ōkubo Toshimichi	1878	Politician
Mori Arinori	1889	Politician
Hoshi Tōru	1901	Politician
Itō Hirobumi	1909	Politician/PM
Hara Takashi	1921	Politician/PM
Yasuda Zenjirō	1921	Business
Hamaguchi Osachi	1931	Politician/PM
Inoue Junnosuke	1932	Business/Politician
Dan Takuma	1932	Business
Inukai Tsuyoshi	1932	Politician/PM
Mutō Sanji	1934	Business/Politician
Nagata Tetsuzan	1935	Army officer
Takahashi Korekiyo	1936	Politician
Saitō Makoto	1936	Navy officer/PM

Note "PM" stands for prime minister
Source Extracted from *Portraits of Modern Japanese Historical Figures*, National Diet Library, Japan, and compiled by the author. www.ndl.go.jp/portrait/e/contents/list.html (accessed on December 11, 2020).

Japanese government maintained close ties with the international financial markets starting from the Russo-Japanese War until Britain's departure from the gold standard. One of its main motivations for returning to the gold standard in 1930, which it succeeded in doing, was to make it easy to refinance a JGB issued in 1905 that was due in 1931. The effective interest rate on the refinanced bond in 1930 was 6.1% (with a coupon of 5.5% at the price of 90/100), which was substantially lower than a loan in 1924 with an effective rate of 7.0% (with a coupon of 6.5% at the price of 92.5) when Japan was off gold. After Britain's departure from the gold standard, however, Japan lost the option of borrowing from foreign investors due to deteriorating conditions in the international financial markets. The return to the gold standard with prudent fiscal and monetary policies was no longer a "good housekeeping seal of approval" (Bordo and Rockoff 1996). At the same time, in the short term, Britain's departure from the gold standard triggered a capital outflow, worsening domestic economic conditions.

Second, the Mukden Incident marked a critical moment when the central government in Tokyo lost control of its army stationed in Manchuria. Japanese troops stationed in territories in Manchuria, known as the Kwantung Army, were supposed to protect the lives and properties of Japanese citizens in those territories following the Russo-Japanese War. On September 18, 1931, the Kwantung Army reported that the Chinese Army had blown up the Manchurian Railway and occupied the main cities alongside the railway. In fact, the reported attack by the Chinese Army was a fake carried out by the Kwantung Army. Suspecting this, the Tokyo government, including the army minister and the army chief of general staff, tried to stop the operations of the Kwantung Army. They failed to do so, however, and eventually had to grant permission for the continuation of the operation *ex post facto*. From this time onward, the army often began operations without the consent of the Tokyo government, and the government was forced to grant permission and pass budgets for such operations *ex post facto* (Banno 2014: 196–199).[6]

In the conventional literature of Japanese political history, the troops in Manchuria have been blamed for the loss of civilian government control of the military. However, recent studies reveal that, in addition to the autocratic behavior of the military itself, another decisive factor behind this loss of governance was the failure of coordination among political players. In particular, it has been revealed that the expansion of the Kwantung Army's operations in the Mukden Incident was ignited by a miscommunication between then foreign minister, Shidehara Kijūrō, and his American counterpart (Inoue 1994, 2012; Banno 2014). Article 11 of the 1889 Meiji Constitution stipulated the "independence of the right of command" of the emperor, which meant the military only followed direct orders from the emperor, not those of the cabinet. Immediately after the outbreak of the Mukden Incident, in response to the remonstration of then US Secretary of State, Henry Stimson, Shidehara send a confidential response to Stimson, stating that the Japanese government had already sent an order for the Kwantung Army to refrain from the expansion of military operations. When Stimson revealed the confidential response to the press, Shidehara and the army chief of general staff lost the confidence of the army in Manchuria for what was considered a violation of the constitutional "independence of the right of command" (Banno 2014: 198). Banno argues that, had the foreign minister explained the delicate issue of the "independence of the right of command" to his American counterpart and asked him not to disclose his confidential report to the press, the army would have followed the order of the Tokyo government.

Then minister of home affairs in the Minseitō Cabinet, Adachi Kenzō, proposed a grand coalition of the two parties, Minseitō and Seiyūkai, to tackle the twin crises of foreign relations and the economy. However, his grand coalition attempt failed due to the opposition of Finance Minister Inoue Junnosuke, who insisted on maintaining of the gold standard, something the opposition Seiyūkai would not agree to (Banno 2014: 199).

On December 13, 1931, the Inukai Tsuyoshi Cabinet was formed as a single-party cabinet by the Seiyūkai. Takahashi returned to office as finance minister, succeeding Inoue, and suspended gold convertibility on the day of his return.

---

[6] In 1928, the Kwantung Army assassinated a Manchurian warlord, Zhang Zuolin, to seize power in Manchuria without consultation with the Tokyo government. This plot, unlike the 1931 Mukden Incident, was not supported by the central government (Nakamura 2012: 108–115).

When he reimposed the gold embargo, Takahashi did not regard the move as a permanent departure from the gold standard (Chap. 3 of this volume). Apparently, he still saw the gold standard as a "good housekeeping seal of approval" (Bordo and Rockoff 1996). Fukai Eigo, Takahashi's adjutant during the Russo-Japanese War and his adviser in the 1930s, later recalled Takahashi's attachment to the gold standard upon the departure from gold: "I was surprised to see Mr. Takahashi still attached to the link between gold and the currency even after reimposing the gold embargo. He seemed uncomfortable about cutting off the institutional link between gold and the currency completely... On the possibility of exchange rate control, he seemed indifferent."[7]

Presumably, Takahashi was not intending to shift either to a flexible exchange rate system, such as the post-Breton Woods system, or to an autarky, such as the illusionary Great East Asia Co-prosperity Sphere, cut off from the rest of the world. While recognizing an overvaluation of the yen under the pre-World War I parity, he intended to maintain links to the international financial markets and tried to be credible in these markets as he had done during the Russo-Japanese War.

The twin crises turned into a triple crisis of foreign relations, the economy, and terrorism. On February 9, 1932, Inoue was assassinated by an ultra-rightwing activist. On May 15, 1932, Prime Minister Inukai was assassinated by a group of navy officers.

Upon the assassination of Inukai, retired admiral Saitō Makoto formed a new grand coalition cabinet. In retrospect, this was the end of the party-based cabinet in prewar Japan. *The Economist* wrote: "How far the two parties will be able to work together and with outsiders, and what the policy of the combination will be, remain in doubt; but there are indications that, if this attempt at a National Government fails, public opinion will be inclined to turn rather to Fascism than to a fresh effort by the parliamentary parties" ("A National Government in Japan," May 28, 1932).

During fiscal 1933 budget negotiations, Takahashi and Prime Minister Sàitō Makoto introduced a top-down approach similar to that in fiscal 1920: the prime minister and finance minister would meet with the army and navy ministers and decide on the military budget ahead of the cabinet meeting. In the process, Takahashi negotiated with Army Minister Araki Sadao and Admiral Okada Keisuke. However, the army at this time demanded a budget increase to deal with "the emergency" in mainland China, and Araki, unlike Tanaka, refused to accept a cut in the military budget. The following year, a formal five-member council comprising the prime minister, the finance minister, the foreign minister, the army minister, and the navy minister was set up for coordinating defense planning and finance. However, Araki and the army ultimately rejected the council's decision, arguing that the army was not bound by the decision Araki had agreed to because of the emperor's right of supreme command over the military. This led to the abandonment of Takahashi's plans for a cabinet-centered process for formulating the national budget (Smethurst 2007: 276–281). In April 1934, Takahashi warned that expenditure, including that for national defense, would have to be cut if the financial markets' capacity to absorb additionally issued government bonds reached its limit (Takahashi 1936b: 58–59).

[7] Fukai (1941: 260–263).

With Japan no longer on the gold standard, the MOF under Takahashi enacted the Capital Flight Prevention Law in 1932 and the Foreign Exchange Control Law in 1933 to regulate capital mobility, thereby facilitating public bond issuance. Even so, he was concerned about fiscal discipline until the very end. In July 1935, seven months before his assassination, he published the following statement in the press:

> Having observed the smooth operation of public bond issuance right since the beginning in 1932, some people argue in favor of an unlimited issuance of public bonds to fund any increase in national expenditure. Such arguments ignore the fact that many states went bankrupt following the Great War.
>
> The smooth operation of public bond issuance so far can be attributed to several factors: (1) an improvement in the government's issuing method, (2) the fact that the volume of bond issuance has been within the absorption capacity of financial institutions in relation to private investments, (3) the fact that this volume has been gradually decreasing, thereby maintaining the credibility of public finance to the people, and (4) the fact that optimal monetary control has achieved price and exchange rate stability, thereby contributing to tremendous recent progress in the country's trade and industry.
>
> Some people circulate ideas that are completely contrary to the government's view, such as that we don't have to be worried about an increase in the volume of national bonds as long as they are issued in the domestic market, because national bonds are both the assets and debts of the citizens of this country. It is only in the accounting statements that assets and debts coexist through national bonds. We cannot be sure that an increase in the volume of national bonds will not hurt fiscal activities and the national economy.
>
> Once the credibility of public finance is lost, national bonds will not be able to be absorbed in the financial markets, and the government will have to rely on a printing machine. Eventually, we will see bad inflation.[8]

Meanwhile the Minseitō and Seiyūkai intensified their mutual tussles rather than cooperate to overcome the crises (Banno 2014: 195). The Seiyūkai even approached the army, supporting its aggression in China. In the midst of this triple crisis, Japan failed to establish a new system for governing fiscal policy, including military spending (Shizume 2018). Takahashi became the last resistor of militarism and guardian of fiscal discipline to be the target of terrorism (Smethurst 2007: 297; Shizume 2011). On September 7, 1935, at the start of budget negotiations and half a year prior to Takahashi's assassination, the *Economist* wrote:

> As the fighting services,... account for more than half of the new charges, and the War Ministry and the Admiralty will not easily acquiesce in any drastic reduction, a hard fight with them over the Defence Estimates is expected. This has impelled Mr. Takahashi, the Finance Minister, to warn both the Cabinet and the public against the danger involved in the deficit-covering loan policy. In a statement which he gave out just before he took a summer vacation he elaborates his standpoint and pours cold water on a growing optimistic belief that the financing of the Budget by borrowing can be pursued indefinitely without bringing about any inflationary effects. With all his vast experience and immense prestige, however, it remains to be seen how far he can stand up to the military chiefs.

On November 30, 1935, Takahashi endured a 21-h cabinet meeting, rejecting an increase in military spending that could not be funded by transfers from other

[8] "A Warning Against Optimism Regarding Deficit Finance: A Statement by the Finance Minister," *Asahi Shimbun*, July 27, 1935, evening edition.

ministries in order to reduce the issue of deficit bonds. The general election of the House of Representatives held on February 20, 1936, six days before his assassination, "gave him a powerful vote of confidence" (Smethurst 2007: 294). This final attempt by Takahashi to maintain fiscal discipline and Japan's "last resistance" to prewar militarism ended with Takahashi's assassination (Smethurst 2007: 298).

References

Banno, Junji. 1992. *The establishment of the Japanese constitutional system*. London; New York: Routledge.

Banno, Junji. 2014. *Japan's modern history, 1857–1937: a new political narrative*. Oxfordshire, England; New York: Routledge.

Bordo, Michael D., and Hugh Rockoff. 1996. The gold standard as a good housekeeping seal of approval. *Journal of Economic History* 56 (2): 389–428.

Bytheway, Simon James. 2014. *Investing Japan: foreign capital, monetary standards, and economic development, 1859–2011*. Cambridge, MA: Harvard East Asia Center, 370.

Doi, Takero, and Tooru Nakazato. 2004. Kōsai no jizoku kanōsei: kuni to chihō no zaisei seido ni sokushita bunseki (Sustainability of public debt: an analysis with reference to the fiscal systems of the national and local governments. Ihori, Toshihiro, ed. *Nihon no zaisei akaji* (Fiscal deficit of Japan), Tokyo: Iwanami Shoten: 53–83.

Ericson, Steven J. 2019. *Financial stabilization in Meiji Japan: the impact of the Matsukata reform*. Ithaca, NY: Cornell University Press.

Fujino, Shōzaburō, and Jūrō Teranishi. 2000. *Nihon kin'yū no sūryō bunseki* (A quantitative analysis of Japanese finance). Tokyo: Tōyō Keizai Shinpōsha.

Fukai, Eigo. 1941. *Kaiko nanajuūnen* (Reflections on the past seventy years). Tokyo: Iwanami Shoten.

He, Wenkai. 2013. *Paths toward the modern fiscal state: England, Japan, and China*. Cambridge, MA: Harvard University Press.

House of Representatives and House of Councilors. 1961. *Gikai seido nanajūnen shi: seitō kaiha hen* (Seventy years of the parliament system: political parties). Tokyo: Ministry of Finance, Printing Bureau.

House of Representatives and House of Councilors. 1962. *Gikai seido nanajūnen shi: shirō hen* (Seventy years of the parliament system: references). Tokyo: Ministry of Finance, Printing Bureau.

Inoue, Toshikazu. 1994. *Kiki no nakano kyōchō gaikō* (Cooperative diplomacy in crisis). Tokyo: Yamakawa Shuppan Sha.

Inoue, Toshikazu. 2012. *Seiyūkai to minseitō* (the Seiyūkai and the Minseitō). Tokyo: Chūkō Shinsho.

Ishibashi, Tanzan. 1921a. Issai o sutsuru no kakugo: Taiheiyō kaigi ni taisuru waga taido (The preparation to abandon everything: the attitude toward the Pacific Conference). *Tōyō Keizai Shinpō* July 23 1921.

Ishibashi, Tanzan. 1921b. Dainihon shugi no gensō (An illusion of the Great Japanism) (1). *Tōyō Keizai Shinpō* July 30 1921.

Ishibashi, Tanzan. 1921c. Dainihon shugi no gensō (An illusion of the Great Japanism) (2). *Tōyō Keizai Shinpō* August 6 1921.

Ishibashi, Tanzan. 1921d. Dainihon shugi no gensō (An illusion of the Great Japanism) (3). *Tōyō Keizai Shinpō* August 13 1921.

Jones, Mark, and Steven Ericson. 2007. Social and economic change in prewar Japan. Tsutsui, William M. ed. *A companion to Japanese history*. Malden, MA: Blackwell: 172–188.

Kamiyama, Tsuneo. 1995. *Meiji Keizai seisaku shi no kenkyū* (A thesis on the economic policy in the Meiji period). Tokyo: Hanawa Shobō.

Kyō, Kokujitsu. 1992. *Ishibashi Tanzan no Shisō shi teki kenkyū* (A thesis on historical aspects of Ishibashi Tanzan's thoughts). Waseda University Press.

Large, Stephan S. 2007. Oligarchy, democracy, and fascism. Tsutsui, William M. ed. *A companion to Japanese history*. Malden, MA: Blackwell Publishing Ltd: 156-171.

Matsusaka, Y. Tak. 2007. The Japanese empire. Tsutsui, William M. ed. *A companion to Japanese History*. Malden, MA: Blackwell Publishing Ltd: 224-240.

Metzler, Mark. 2006. *Lever of empire: the international gold standard and the crisis of liberalism in prewar Japan*. Berkeley and Los Angeles: University of California Press.

Ministry of Finance. 1936. *Meiji-Taishō zaisei shi 11: kokusai1* (The financial history of the Meiji-Taishō periods 11: national debt 1). Tokyo: Zaisei Keizai Gakkai.

Ministry of Finance. 1954. *Shōwa zaisei shi 6: kokusai* (The financial history of the Shōwa period 6: national debt). Tokyo: Tōyō Keizai Shinpōsha.

Ministry of Finance. 1955. *Shōwa zaisei shi 4: rinji gunjihi* (The financial history of the Shōwa period 4: temporary military spending). Tokyo: Tōyō Keizai Shinpōsha.

Ministry of Finance. Various issues. Kinyū jikō sankō sho (Reference book of financial matters). Tokyo: Ministry of Finance.

Mitani, Hiroshi. 1997. *Meiji ishin to nashonarizumu* (The Meiji Restoration and nationalism). Tokyo: Yamakawa Shuppan sha.

Mitani, Hiroshi. 2013. *Aikoku, kakumei, minshu* (Patriotism, revolution and democracy). Tokyo: Chikuma Sensho.

Mitani, Hiroshi. 2017. *Ishin shi saikō: Kōgi, ōsei kara Shūken, datsu mibunka e.* (Revisiting history of the Meiji Restoration: from public debate under the imperial rule to a concentration of power being free from the class society). Tokyo: NHK Books.

Mitchener, Kris James, Masato Shizume, and Marc D. Weidenmier. 2010a. Why did countries adopt the gold standard? Lessons from Japan. *Journal of Economic History* 70 (1): 27–56.

Mitchener, Kris James, and Marc D. Weidenmier. 2010b. Supersanctions and sovereign debt repayment. *Journal of International Money and Finance* 29: 19–36.

Mosk, Carl. 2007. *Japanese economic development: markets, norms, structures*. London: Routledge.

Nakamura, Takafusa. 2012. *Shōwa shi* (A history of the Shōwa period), 1. Tokyo: Tōyō Keizai Shinpōsha.

Ohkawa, Kazushi, and Miyohei Shinohara. 1979. *Patterns of Japanese economic development: a quantitative appraisal*. New Haven, CT: Yale University Press.

Ohkawa, Kazushi, Nobukiyo Takamatsu, and Yūzō Yamamoto. 1974. *Estimates of long-term economic statistics of Japan since 1868, 1, national income*. Tokyo: Tōyō Keizai Shinpōsha.

Shizume, Masato. 2009. *Sekai kyōkō to keizai seisaku: kaihō shōkoku nihon no keiken to gendai* (The world depression and economic policy: lessons from Japan as a small open economy). Tokyo: Nikkei shinbun shuppan sha.

Shizume, Masato. 2011. Sustainability of public debt: evidence from Japan before the second world war. *Economic History Review* 64–4: 1113–1143.

Shizume, Masato. 2018. A history of the Bank of Japan, 1882–2016. Jacobson, Tor, Daniel Waldenström, and Rodney Edvinsson eds. *Sveriges Riksbank 350 years: a central bank in a world of central banks*. Cambridge, UK: Cambridge University Press: 328–360.

Smethurst, Richard J. 2007. *From foot soldier to finance minister: Takahashi Korekiyo, Japan's Keynes*. Cambridge, MA: Harvard University Asia Center, 292.

Suzuki, Toshio. 1994. *Japanese government loan issues on the London capital market, 1870–1913*. London; Atlantic Highlands, NJ: Athlone Press.

Takahashi, Korekiyo. 1936a. *Zuisōroku* (Memoir). Tokyo: Chikura Shobō.

Takahashi, Korekiyo. 1936b. Keizairon (Economics). Tokyo: Chikura Shobō.

Chapter 5
Origins of the Economic Ideas of Takahashi Korekiyo

In this chapter, I will explore the origins of Takahashi's policies with reference to his career and personal networks in a global context both in time and space. I will begin with the development of his career, which informed his perception of society and the economy. Then, I will review his accomplishments as finance minister from his first appointment in 1913 through 1936, when he was assassinated. Finally, I will summarize his thoughts in relation to his earlier career and experience.

5.1 Development of Takahashi's Career

Takahashi was born in Edo (now Tokyo) in 1854, the year following Commodore Perry's first visit to Japan, which was also the year in which the Treaty of Peace and Amity between the United States and Japan was concluded.[1] He was assassinated in 1936, the year before the Marco Polo Bridge Incident, which marked the outbreak of the Second Sino-Japanese War. In this sense, he lived through eight decades of Japan's modernization as part of its globalization efforts from the second half of the nineteenth century through most of the first half of the twentieth century (Table 5.1).

Smethurst's seminal work (Smethurst 2007) offers a detailed account in English of Takahashi's life. Other literature related to Takahashi in English includes Metzler (2006), which discusses Japan's modernization with reference to money and finance in the global context. Based on these works and other related materials, I will briefly review Takahashi's career, focusing on the formation of his thoughts on economic policy.

[1] Takahashi was the illegitimate child of an official painter of the Tokugawa Shogun and was adopted as a baby by a low-ranking samurai (*ashigaru*, or "foot soldier") of the Sendai Domain who worked as gatekeeper for the domain's Edo office (Smethurst 2007: 9–13).

M. Shizume, *The Japanese Economy During the Great Depression*,
Studies in Economic History,
https://doi.org/10.1007/978-981-13-7357-2_5

Table 5.1 Biography of Takahashi Korekiyo

Year	Event	Concurrent event in the larger world
1854	Born in Edo	US–Japan Treaty of Peace and Amity
1864–1865	Studies English in Yokohama	
1866–1867	Works in the house of a Scottish banker, Alexander Allan Shand	
1867–1868	Ventures on a trip to the United States	Meiji Restoration (1868)
1869	Teaches English at the Daigaku Nankō	
1871	Teaches at the Karatsu English Language School	
1873	Joins the Ministry of Education	
1876	Teaches at the Tokyo English Language School	
1881	Joins the Ministry of Agriculture and Commerce	Establishment of the BOJ (1882)
1885–1886	Travels to the United States and Europe to study trademark and patent laws	
1889–1890	Travels to Peru to run a silver mine	Establishment of the Meiji Constitution (1889), the first session of the Japanese parliament (1890)
1892	Joins the BOJ	
1893–1895	Becomes manager of the BOJ's Saibu branch	The First Sino-Japanese War (1894–1895)
1895–1897	Becomes the general manager of the Yokohama Specie Bank	
1897–1899	Becomes the vice president of the Yokohama Specie Bank	
1898	Travels to Britain and the United States	
1899–1911	Becomes the deputy governor of the BOJ	
1904–1905 1906–1907	Travels to Europe and the United States to raise funds for the Russo-Japanese War; becomes a member of the House of Peers (1905)	The Russo-Japanese War (1904–1905)
1911–1913	Becomes the governor of the BOJ	
1913–1914	Joins the Seiyūkai (1913); becomes finance minister of the Yamamoto cabinet	World War I (1914–1918)
1918–1921	Becomes finance minister of the Hara cabinet	The assassination of Prime Minister Hara (1921)
1921–1922	Becomes the prime minister while concurrently serving as the finance minister	The Washington Naval Conference

(continued)

Table 5.1 (continued)

Year	Event	Concurrent event in the larger world
1924–1925	Becomes a member of the House of representatives and the agriculture and commerce minister of the Katō Cabinet	The Great Kantō Earthquake (1923)
1927	Becomes finance minister of the Tanaka Cabinet	The Shōwa financial crisis
1931–1932	Becomes finance minister of the Inukai Cabinet	Departure from the gold standard, the Mukden Incident (1931), the May 15 Incident (1932)
1932–1934	Becomes finance minister of the Saitō Cabinet	
1934–1936	Becomes finance minister of the Okada Cabinet	
1936	Assassinated	The February 26 Incident

Source Smethurst (2007)

When Takahashi first joined the Meiji Government in the early 1870s, he was recognized as an English-language expert because of his outstanding spoken English skills acquired during his teen years. Takahashi first learned to speak English in Yokohama at the age of ten, from Clarissa Hepburn, wife of a missionary called James Hepburn. Subsequently, he worked for Alexander Allan Shand, the acting manager of the Yokohama branch of the Chartered Mercantile Bank of London, China, and India. Later, he was selected by the domain government to study in the United States. However, he was unable to obtain any formal education upon arrival at San Francisco, either due to some miscommunication with his host or by a malevolent intention of the mediator. Instead, he was forced to work as a servant for a local family. Thanks to his outgoing and uninhibited personality, he managed to survive on his own in the local community and acquired outstanding spoken English and negotiating skills as a result of this extraordinary experience for a young Japanese during this period (Smethurst 2007: 18–32).

After working in several public- and private-sector positions, Takahashi received his first professional training as an economic bureaucrat when he joined the Ministry of Agriculture and Commerce in 1881. He worked under Maeda Masana, an advocate for development policy with emphasis on the promotion of a civilian economy. Takahashi worked on a project to draft proposals for the promotion of industry (*kōgyō iken*) submitted in 1884. The original draft of the report emphasized improving productivity in agriculture and traditional industries, and promoting exports and import substitution. Maeda also proposed the establishment of a development bank to promote regional industrial development. The proposals triggered an intense debate between proponents and opponents, including Finance Minister Matsukata Masayoshi, who preferred a more centralized economic development with emphasis on heavy industry. Eventually, Maeda's proposals were effectively dismissed or watered down (Smethurst 2007: 79–95, Column of this Chap. 5.8 Maeda Masana, Matsukata Masayoshi, and the French Connection).

After joining the BOJ in 1892, Takahashi became an active member of the financial and banking community. In 1899, he was appointed deputy governor of the BOJ and, in 1904, upon the outbreak of the Russo-Japanese War, he concurrently became the financial commissioner for war financing. His excellent English-language skills, especially his ability to speak fluently and negotiate effectively, his experience working with the financial and banking community, and his personality as an open-minded but tough negotiator were some of the reasons leaders in the government appointed him to this position, which marked a turning point both for his career and his economic ideas (Smethurst 2007:141).

Takahashi traveled to London, New York, and continental Europe to raise funds for the war, where he consulted and negotiated with prominent Western financiers on a series of sovereign loans. He regularly presented his views on Japan's financial condition and the government's capacity to repay debts to the media. He also sent many cables and letters back to the Japanese government and central bank, reporting on the views of Western investors and offering his own economic and foreign policy advice.

Takahashi warned the Tokyo government of the need for a prudent fiscal policy, in a cable to the BOJ governor Matsuo Shigeyoshi when he negotiated on the condition of bond issuance with bankers in London in September 1905 after the ceasefire (Chap. 4 of this volume, Smethurst 2007: 183).

Takahashi's achievements were remarkable. The Russo-Japanese War cost the Japanese government 1.9 billion yen, almost six times the central government's total spending in 1903. Forty percent of the expense was financed by foreign loans (Metzler 2006: 43). Japan could not have fought the war with Russia without Takahashi. Following the war, Takahashi came to be recognized as an emerging leader in Japanese financial policy, and the emperor appointed him as a member of the House of Peers in 1905.

During his time in Europe and North America, Takahashi established an extensive network of connections with Western financiers. Key among these connections was Jacob Schiff, senior partner in Kuhn, Loeb & Co., one of New York's two great investment banks, comparable only to J. P. Morgan.[2] Takahashi and Schiff established a close friendship from their first meeting in London in May 1904, when Schiff proposed underwriting the first issue of Japan's overseas war bond. Schiff was seven years older than Takahashi and became a mentor to him in the financial world as well as being an extremely reliable business partner. Takahashi's daughter lived with Schiff's family during her studies in the United States (Smethurst 2006: 149–165).

[2] Schiff was born into a middle-class Jewish family in Frankfurt in 1847, emigrated to New York as a teenager in 1865, and had become one of the richest and most powerful financiers in America by 1904 (Smethurst 2007: 149–150).

5.2 Takahashi as Finance Minister

After serving as governor of the BOJ during 1911–1913 (Fig. 5.1), Takahashi joined the Seiyūkai to become finance minister in the Yamamoto Gonnohyōe Cabinet. Starting then, he served as finance minister a total of five times in seven cabinets from 1913 to 1936 (Table 5.2). His time in office as finance minister added up to a total of nine years.

Takahashi entered politics when Japan was transitioning from the old political system characterized by an administrative branch led by the Satsuma–Chōshū clique and political parties representing taxpayers, consisting of landowners and merchants, to a new, two-party system comprising the conservative Seiyūkai party and the liberal Kenseikai-Minseitō party, both based on elected seats in the House of Representatives. The Yamamoto Cabinet was formed in the vortex of the mass "movement to preserve a constitutional government." Although Yamamoto was from the Satsuma faction, the Seiyūkai backed his cabinet as the ruling party, and Takahashi joined the party to become the finance minister (Metzler 2006: 85–87; Banno 2014: 146–151).

During Takahashi's first term in 1913–1914, Japan's fiscal and monetary policies were constrained by the burden of servicing the Russo-Japanese War debt. In terms of the balance of payments, a current account deficit persisted, and foreign reserves continued to fall. International investors were worried about the capacity of Japan to repay its debts. Takahashi sought to issue foreign bonds for national railway construction and the refinancing of existing loans. However, the government could

Fig. 5.1 Takahashi as governor of the BOJ. *Source* From the website of governors of the BOJ, by courtesy of the Bank of Japan: www.boj.or.jp/en/about/outline/history/pre_gov/sousai07.htm/

Table 5.2 Takahashi's terms as finance minister

Start	End	Prime Minister	Events in Japan	World events
February 20, 1913	April 16, 1914	Yamamoto Gonnohyōe	Reserve shortage, constitutional movement	Establishment of the Republic of China (1912)
September 29, 1918	June 12, 1922	Hara Takashi, Takahashi Korekiyo	Gold embargo (1917), rice riots (1918), the great influenza pandemic (1918–1920), financial panic (1920)	World War I (1914–1918), the treaty of versailles (1919), the Washington Naval conference (1921–1922)
April 20, 1927	June 2, 1927	Tanaka Giichi	The Showa financial crisis (1927)	
December 13, 1931	July 8, 1934	Inukai Tsuyoshi, Saitō Makoto	Lifting of the gold embargo (1930), the Mukden incident (1931), departure from the gold standard (1931), the May 15 incident (1932), the start of BOJ underwriting JGBs (1932)	Black Thursday (1929), Britain's departure from the gold standard (1931), US departure from the gold standard (1933)
November 27, 1934	February 26, 1936	Okada Keisuke	The February 26 incident (assassination of Takahashi) (1936)	

Source Nihon Kinyū Nenpyō (1993)

not issue long-term bonds. Takahashi was allowed little discretion to implement an expansionary policy and was forced to implement retrenchment in fiscal policy (Metzler 2006: 87–88). Takahashi's first term was cut short by the cabinet's resignation *en masse* following the Siemens-Vickers Scandal related to the procurement of a battlecruiser by naval officers. Japan remained perched on the edge of a foreign debt crisis cliff until World War I reversed external trade and financial conditions in Japan's favor.

Takahashi returned to office as finance minister of the Hara Takashi Cabinet in 1918, the last year of World War I, to a scenario completely different from the one at the time of his resignation on the eve of the war. Japan was now posting current account surpluses thanks to the steady growth in exports, and its foreign reserves had accumulated. The country had gone from being indebted to the rest of the world to becoming an international creditor. Meanwhile, it had also implemented a gold embargo following in the footsteps of the Unites States in 1917.

Hara's Seiyūkai came to power with a manifesto comprising four goals: to strengthen national defense, to encourage education, to promote industry, and to develop a transportation system. Takahashi formulated an expansionary budget for fiscal 1920 to achieve these goals. He rejected proposals to lift the gold embargo for strategic reasons, namely, to use the accumulating foreign reserves for investments in China rather than hold them for maintaining the gold standard (Metzler 2006: 118–124).[3]

In September 1920, Takahashi tried to circulate a proposal to abolish the Army General Staff Office (Chap. 4 of this volume). Hara stopped the attempt because Takahashi's idea was too progressive and not feasible under current political circumstances (Smethurst 2007: 220; Banno 2014: 170–171). Smethurst (2007: 211) argues that Takahashi had already developed a coherent view of the role of national defense in the context of foreign and economic policy. In brief, his view was that defense planning ought not to hinder economic growth.

When Hara was shot to death in 1921, Takahashi succeeded him as the head of the Seiyūkai and became the prime minister. During this time, Takahashi served concurrently as both prime minister and finance minister. His biggest accomplishment as prime minister was the conclusion of the Washington Naval Disarmament Treaty in February 1922. However, the Takahashi Cabinet collapsed in June 1922 over disagreements regarding Takahashi's proposal to cut defense spending as a means of fiscal retrenchment. Several principal members of the cabinet opposed Takahashi's proposal because they regarded it as contradicting the party's goal of enhancing national defense as stated in the manifesto formulated under Hara's leadership. Smethurst argues: "Takahashi failed as prime minister and leader of the Seiyūkai not only because he lacked Hara's skills in dealing with party members, but also because he proposed a platform that challenged long-standing party policies and threatened the party's support bases, regardless of how forward-looking and rational the platform appears in retrospect" (Smethurst 2007: 230).

Despite having decided to retire from politics, Takahashi was asked to return office in the midst of the Showa Financial Crisis of 1927.[4] He declared a moratorium and

---

[3] In sharp contrast to the measures taken against COVID-19 in the twenty-first century, Takahashi did not prioritize countermeasures against the influenza pandemic of 1918–1920 (Shizume 2021).

[4] The seeds of the crisis were sown in the boom years during and immediately after World War I. In the subsequent adjustment process in the early-mid 1920s, the final resolution to the bad debt problem was postponed. To deal with the huge physical loss due to the Great Kantō Earthquake of 1923, the government and the BOJ introduced a rescue program, *shinsai tegata*, or the earthquake bill facility, which postponed repayment deadlines for banks and companies in the devastated area. It was perceived as a temporary measure, and the deadline was first set for March 1925, but later extended twice up to September 1927. When the government decided to finally end the earthquake bill facility, it was revealed that unsettled earthquake bills were consolidated within a single drawer–accepter pair: drawn by Suzuki and Company, an emerging trading company based in Kobe and engaged in exports of sugar and camphor from Taiwan, and accepted by the Bank of Taiwan, a public institution in charge of note issuance and commercial finance in Taiwan. Both these companies had offices in the devastated Kantō area. The fact was that Suzuki misused the earthquake bill facility to cover up its bad debts resulting from speculative activities during and after World War I. The revelation led the opposition Seiyūkai to attack the ruling Kenseikai Wakatsuki Cabinet for rescuing

implemented emergency measures including a liquidity provision through the BOJ's lender of last resort (LOLR) function to quell the panic (Shizume 2018b). Having overseen the country's return to financial stability in 40 days, he decided once again to retire from political life at the age of 74 (Smethurst 2007: 233–237).

However, he once again accepted the role of finance minister in December 1931, at the age of 77, and went on to orchestrate the remarkable economic recovery outlined in Chaps. 1 through 3 of this volume. Takahashi had experienced a life as a commoner on the west coast of the United States as well as in Japan and learned on the job the essence of development and macroeconomic policies for a small, open economy in the international financial markets. He had already established a reputation as a charismatic financial statesman who could rescue Japan from crisis.

Apart from the practical training related above, Takahashi had also learned a great deal from books, newspapers, and magazines, and through his conversations with opinion leaders both in Japan and in the English-speaking world. Smethurst (2007: 306) argues that, by the interwar years, educated Japanese were no longer living in an exotic "backwater" far from the European and North American "center." Takahashi was, therefore, very much a part of the mainstream of global intellectual elites.

5.3 Principles of Takahashi's Economic Policies

Now, we are ready to discuss Takahashi's economic policy ideas and their origins. To understand Takahashi's economic policies in the early 1930s, we need to put them in their historical, global, and politico-economic contexts. His policy ideas for tackling the crisis cannot be understood simply by looking at the period in question. We need to explore his lifetime experience, both domestic and international, and his contemplations based on this experience. At the same time, his achievements should not be evaluated as an experiment in a clean laboratory or as a textbook example of economic theory. Takahashi had to conduct policy with an eclectic pragmatism in the real world with uncertainties and constraints in terms of economic, political, and social conditions.

In December 1921, when Takahashi became prime minister, he wrote a short essay titled "For National Wealth," declaring, "The ultimate goal of politics and economics is to enhance the welfare of the people in both the present and the future." To achieve this goal, he continued, "it is essential for people to have wealth, see improvements in their living standards, thereby gaining a greater sense of well-being, and be able to exercise their intellectual abilities to the fullest in producing life's basic necessities inexpensively" (Takahashi 1936b: 119).

In practice, Takahashi's economic policies had three goals: (1) to achieve full employment, (2) to facilitate economic growth by promoting investment to expand

a specific company using taxpayer money. When Wakatsuki resigned, Tanaka Giichi, a retired army general and the next head of Seiyūkai after Takahashi, came to power. It was Tanaka who asked Takahashi to solve the problem and restore financial order (Shizume 2018b).

production capacity and improve productivity, and (3) to maintain credibility in the international financial markets in the long run.[5]

5.4 Takahashi's Policies for Achieving Full Employment

For Takahashi, the first goal of achieving full employment meant not only producing to the best of physical and human capacity on an aggregate level, but also fully utilizing the ability of individual workers to earn their living. In other words, he took the commoner's perspective as his starting point and was concerned about the daily lives of individual workers.

Takahashi took a pragmatic approach to the gold standard in that he admitted its usefulness as a governance mechanism but was not a hostage to the ideology dubbed the "golden fetters" (Eichengreen 1992). In a magazine article in November 1929, he used the impressive analogy of a geisha house to elaborate on the Keynesian multiplier effect mechanism seven years before Keynes' *The General Theory of Employment, Interest and Money* was published (Takahashi 1936a: 247–252):

> To put it plainly, if a person goes to a geisha house and spends 2,000 yen on a sumptuous meal and the services of a geisha, we disapprove morally. But if we analyze how that money is used, we find that the portion paid for food helps support the chef's salary, the portion used for purchasing and transporting fish, meat, vegetables, and seasonings are paid to the supplying merchants, who in turn provide income to farmers and fishermen. The farmers, fishermen, and merchants use the money they receive to buy food, clothes, and shelter. The geisha uses her portion of the money to buy food, clothes, and cosmetics, and to pay taxes.
>
> Supposing the hypothetical man in our example were to save his 2,000 yen instead of going to a geisha house, his bank deposit would grow, but the efficacy of his money would be lessened. However, he does go to a geisha house, and the money is transferred into the hands of farmers, artisans, and fishermen. From there, it goes to various other producers and workers twenty or thirty times over.
>
> From an individual's point of view, it would be good to save 2,000 yen, but from the vantage point of the national economy, spending is better, because it allows the money to work twenty or thirty times over. This is where an individual's budget and the national economy differ.
>
> The example I have given is an extreme one. I am not encouraging people to go to geisha houses or to borrow money to live beyond their means. The point I wish to make is simply that what is good for the individual and what is good for the nation are different.

Takahashi then went on to criticize the Hamaguchi Government for its constrictive fiscal policies in preparation for lifting the gold embargo:

> No matter how much we praise individual frugality, we cannot applaud a national policy that weakens Japan's industrial power. Adopting a restrictive fiscal policy means constraining new governmental spending. The finance minister cancelled several projects already begun…

---

[5] Smethurst (2007: 299–300) outlines 13 of Takahashi's economic policy principles. My three elements of Takahashi's economic policy goals are an abstract of these economic principles as compiled by Smethurst (2007). I have excluded Takahashi's political and social policy principles, such as promoting wider political participation and a decentralized education system.

> When the government stopped work on these projects, builders lost their contracts. They in turn laid off clerks, engineers, and construction workers, and ended their contracts with suppliers of the required materials and merchants in general. All these people are victims of government frugality.
>
> The people who lost their jobs lost disposable income. The workers' reduced buying power was passed on to their suppliers and other people not directly involved in the construction work in question. They too laid off workers, leading to further production cuts. As a result, the government's policies invited general recession.

Some observers indicate that Takahashi was inspired by Keynes' work predating his *General Theory*. Nanto and Takagi (1985: 372) point to an influential pamphlet Keynes coauthored with Hubert Henderson in 1929 entitled "Can Lloyd George Do It?" and suggests that "it is quite likely that [Takahashi] had read the Keynesian description of [the expenditure multiplier] by 1929." In this regard, in an article on May 1, 1929, five months before Takahashi's remark, Keynes (1929) had discussed the effects of the public works program proposed by Lloyd George of the Liberal Party, stating:

> There is nothing fanciful or fine-spun about the proposition that the construction of roads entails a demand for road materials, which entails a demand for labour and also for other commodities, which, in their turn, entail a demand for labour… That a demand for a suit of clothes implies a demand for cloth; that a demand for cloth implies a demand for yearns and tops, and so for wool; that the services of farmers, merchants, engineers, miners, transport workers, clerks, are all involved—this is the A B C of economic science.
>
> Generally speaking, the indirect employment which schemes of capital expenditure would entail is far larger than the direct employment.

However, there is no evidence that Takahashi had read Keynes' article in *The Nation*. Smethurst (2007: 305–306) concludes that "it is unclear when and from where he developed the idea that the government could use deficit fiscal spending to stimulate demand, particularly during economic downturns."

Although Takahashi's policy of using government spending to achieve this goal has been often credited to the "Keynesian" nature of his economic thought, the fact is that Takahashi's ideas originated from Masana Maeda's concept of grass-roots economic development in his 1884 proposals for the promotion of industry. In the original draft of *Opinions on the Promotion of Industry*, Maeda advocated the development of regional and traditional enterprise before imported heavy industry by providing local producers. Maeda intended to raise rural standards of living and create wealth as a foundation for the later development of the heavy industry. Maeda criticized Finance Minister Matsukata Masayoshi's austerity policy as "running a child off a cliff" (Smethurst 2007: 88–89, 305–306). Takahashi's argument in favor of a stimulus for local production and his critique of the Hamaguchi Government's retrenchment measures in 1929 echoed Maeda's critique of Matsukata in 1884.

5.5 Takahashi's Policies for Facilitating Economic Growth by Promoting Investment

Takahashi's second economic policy goal of facilitating economic growth by promoting investment to expand production capacity and improve productivity related to his view on the mechanism of economic growth and the distribution of wealth. He emphasized two factors as the main sources of economic growth—the improvement of product quality and the expansion of production capacity through greater production process efficiency. While he referenced Adam Smith and Friedrich List in this context (Takahashi 1936b: 8–10), it is conceivable that he was also influenced by Alfred Marshall, whose work he had translated into Japanese in his youth (Smethurst 2007: 57).[6]

Sometime around 1925, Takahashi wrote an essay titled "How Does National Production Grow?" In this essay, he explained the mechanism of economic growth and policy goals under the new state of international competition:

> Four key factors contribute to growth in national production: entrepreneurship for risk-taking, good management for controlling the production process, capital, and labor. National wealth is created through the integration of these four factors.
>
> Today, in Europe and America, when competition among countries has shifted from the military sphere to the economic sphere as a result of disarmament, leaders are inspiring their people toward four economic goals – first, to increase the quantity and improve the quality of products; second, to increase wages for workers; third, achieve greater profits from business activities; and fourth, achieve lower prices through improved productivity.

The natural policy recommendation derived from these notions was to promote low interest rates. Low interest rates would lower the cost of investment and stimulate capital accumulation. Low interest rates would decrease the capital share of income and increase the labor share. Takahashi, citing the higher interest rates in Japan relative to foreign (Western) countries, called for the interest rates to be lowered:

> Today in this country, even esteemed borrowers have to pay an interest of eight percent or more, though this is lower than before. Ordinary industrialists have to pay ten to fifteen percent. Their counterparts in foreign countries only pay five to seven percent. In foreign countries, the burden of capital cost on production is half that in Japan…
>
> Lowering interest rates for the business community is a matter of utmost urgency… Interest is added to production costs… Bringing down Japanese interest rates by five to seven percent would greatly alleviate the burden on working people, such as merchants and industrialists, in their efforts to create national wealth.[7]

Takahashi had made consistent efforts to lower domestic interest rates to the extent possible right from his days in the BOJ. Twice, he resisted the attempts of

---

[6] Smethurst reveals that Marshall sent Takahashi a letter of thanks for the translation, which Takahashi still had in his possession in the 1930s.

[7] Takahashi (1936a: 353–356). The date of the original script is unknown, but going by the other parts of the text, it is assumed to be from around 1925. Takahashi wrote another piece echoing this economic viewpoint in October 1925 titled "On the Principle of Economics: For the Industries of This Country." (Takahashi 1936b: 3–32).

his colleague Yamamoto Tatsuo, an advocate for sound money, to raise the BOJ's official interest rate—once in 1899–1900, when Yamamoto was the governor and Takahashi the deputy governor of the BOJ, and again in 1911, when Yamamoto was the finance minister and Takahashi was the governor of the BOJ (Smethurst 2007: 138–139, 201). Finally, in the early 1930s, Takahashi was able to pursue his low interest rate policy without hindrance.

At the same time, he urged capitalists to share the fruits of economic growth with workers. In an October 1925 article titled "On the Principle of Economics: For the Industries of This Country," he stated:

> If productivity improves, capitalists should share the pie of reduced cost of production with workers and consumers. If a factory is now able to make something with six workers which it previously made with ten workers, the manager should share the cost reduction with workers by raising their wages by the equivalent of two workers' previous wages, and with consumers by reducing the price of products by the equivalent of the other two workers' previous wages.

In sum, Takahashi viewed monetary policy as a policy instrument not only to stimulate aggregate demand but also to enhance the supply side of the economy through investments.

5.6 Takahashi's Policies for Maintaining the Credibility of State Finance

While the first and second goals described above represent the lenient side of Takahashi's economic policy principles, the third goal of maintaining credibility in the international financial markets represents the disciplinary aspect of his macroeconomic policy in the long run. As we have seen in a previous section of this chapter, it is conceivable that he acquired this idea during his years in the banking sector, especially his visits to Europe and North America to negotiate on Japanese government bond issuance for funding the Russo-Japanese War.

When he reimposed the gold embargo in December 1931, Takahashi did not regard the move as a permanent departure from the gold standard. Apparently, he saw the gold standard as a "good housekeeping seal of approval" (Bordo and Rockoff 1996).

From the viewpoint of fiscal discipline, the biggest challenge in pre-World War II Japan was the management of military spending (Shizume 2018a). Alongside his radical idea of integrating the military by abolishing the Army General Staff Office, Takahashi also continued trying to build a scheme for negotiation within the administrative branch in a pragmatic manner, which worked in the 1920s but not in the 1930s. He recognized the importance of the authorities having a "dialogue with the financial market," as he mentioned in conversations with Fukai (1941: 269). During negotiations with the military, he used signals from the financial markets as warnings of deteriorating fiscal discipline.

5.7 How Takahashi Dealt with the Macroeconomic Policy Trilemma

The macroeconomic policy trilemma (or "the impossible trinity") posits that no macroeconomic policy regime can succeed in achieving more than two out of the three policy objectives of (1) independent monetary policy oriented toward domestic objectives, (2) fixed exchange rates, and (3) full freedom of cross-border capital movements.[8]

Takahashi's contemporaries during the interwar period, including policymakers and market participants, fully understood the concept of the macroeconomic policy trilemma. BOJ governor Hijikata Hisaakira stated at a branch managers' meeting in May 1931, when Japan returned to the gold standard, that the central bank was sacrificing the domestic economy to defend the gold parity while maintaining the free movement of capital under the gold standard.[9]

Takahashi's solution was a drastic one-shot devaluation of the yen to a new equilibrium that would also give him substantial space for fiscal and monetary policy stimulus. As I have shown in previous chapters, he did not intend to switch to a floating exchange rate system. Even so, he fully used the capacity of the MOF and the BOJ to stimulate the domestic economy while maintaining exchange rate stability. At the same time, despite having introduced a scheme of capital control, he held back on regulations, ensuring that they were only sufficient to curb speculative attacks on the yen, not to restrain international trade activities (Shizume 2009a: 77–79, 2009b: 8).[10]

5.8 Column: Maeda Masana, Matsukata Masayoshi, and the French Connection

In the Meiji period, Japanese policymakers often traveled to Europe and the United States to study modern technologies and systems. In the case of Maeda Masana and Matsukata Masayoshi, traveling to France marked turning points for them. Both of them traveled in the 1870s, but acquired somewhat different knowledge.

---

[8] Obstfeld and Taylor (2004) apply the concept of the macroeconomic policy trilemma in a comparative historical framework to explore the relationship between the currency system and monetary policy in a number of countries during the pre-World War II period. They argue that the gold standard was a typical policy regime designed to maintain free capital movement and a fixed exchange rate while sacrificing independent monetary policy.

[9] "Branch Managers' Meeting Spring–Fall 1931," BOJ Archives, No. 3942, cited by Shizume (2009a: 73–74).

[10] A few other countries, such as Sweden and Denmark, chose options similar to Japan's. They departed from the gold standard following Britain, depreciated their currencies against the pound sterling, and achieved economic recovery earlier than other European countries during the Great Depression (Eichengreen 1992: 298–309).

Maeda Masana (1850–1921) was born in the Satsuma Domain to a medical doctor. He studied in France from 1869 to 1877 under the tutelage of Eugène Tisserand (1830–1925), deputy minister of the French Ministry of Agriculture and Commerce and an agricultural technocrat (Smethurst 2007: 84; Soda 2017: 260–262). Maeda survived the Franco-Prussian War (1870–1871) and Paris Commune (1871) during his stay in Paris. When the French government planned the third Paris World's Fair in 1878 (the Exposition Universelle) to showcase its recovery from defeat in war and political turbulence, Maeda proposed that the Japanese government use this opportunity to promote Japanese products and culture, and his proposal was accepted. He briefly returned to Japan in 1877, carrying plants and seeds that he thought would be useful for Japanese agriculture, then went back to Paris as the secretary general of the Japanese delegate to the expo, in which Tisserand served as director of the agriculture, horticulture, and fish farming section.

Eugène Tisserand, Maeda's mentor in France, was not a well-known figure in France. He was born in Flavigny-sur-Moselle (in the northeast of France) to Louis Tisserand, baker and then royal gendarme in Flavigny-sur-Moselle and knight of the Legion of Honor. After studying agronomics in the early 1850s, Eugène traveled to and lived in other parts of Europe including England, Scotland, Belgium, Holland, Denmark, Sweden, Norway, Germany, Switzerland, Austria, Hungary, Romania, Italy, and Spain for research on the practice of agriculture. He returned to work for agricultural development and was appointed inspector general of agriculture in 1871, deputy director of agriculture at the Ministry of Agriculture and Trade in 1874, director of the National Agronomic Institute when it was reconstituted in 1876, and director of agriculture in 1879. Alongside his administrative work for the French government, Tisserand worked on projects related to international agricultural exhibitions. In the Exposition Universelle, in which Maeda served as the secretary general of the Japanese delegate, Tisserand organized several exhibitions, including one of new agricultural machinery. He also wrote a number of books on practical issues related to agriculture and served as the French government's delegate to the International Statistical Commission in Stockholm in 1874 (Court of Audit (France) website, publication date unknown).

Maeda's career as a technocrat in the agricultural development traced that of his mentor, Tisserand. His economic ideas were also influenced by Tisserand's own. While politically conservative, opposing liberal democracy, he believed the primary goal of economic policy was to raise the living standards of ordinary people. As in France, the majority of the Japanese population also lived in rural areas, so Maeda advocated a bottom-up approach of economic development based on improvements in productivity and the expansion of markets for agriculture and indigenous industries, and opposed a top-down approach based on heavy industries with imported technologies. Presumably, Maeda accepted Tisserand's conceptual framework toward regional development based on growth in agriculture and indigenous industries as a standard for Japanese modernization.

Matsukata Masayoshi (1835–1924) was born in the Satsuma Domain to a samurai. After his participation in the Boshin Civil War of 1868–1869 against the Tokugawa Shogunate, he was appointed the governor of Hita Prefecture (in Kyūshū in southwest

Japan) in 1868 and then joined the MOF in 1871. He went on to work for the ministry throughout the rest of his career, and holds the record as the longest serving finance minister. After Ōkuma Shigenobu was ousted from the ministry, Matsukata served as finance minister from October 1881 to August 1892, from March to August 1895, from September 1896 to January 1898, and November 1898 to October 1900. As finance minister, he established the BOJ in 1882 and introduced the silver and gold standards in 1885 and 1897, respectively. During his early days as finance minister, Matsutaka adopted an austerity policy, which, it is believed, resulted in severe economic contraction and deflation (Ericson 2019).

Matsukata traveled to Europe as the deputy director of the Japanese government to the Exposition Universelle, while the director, Ōkubo Toshimichi, stayed back in Japan, meaning that Matsukata was the de facto head of the Japanese delegation and Maeda's supervisor. Matsutaka made good use of the opportunity of his appointment as deputy director to the Exposition Universelle to tour western Europe, traveling to Britain, Germany, Switzerland, the Netherlands, and France, to investigate their financial, economic, and transportation systems and to meet with scholars and officials. Among other things, he took on the important mission of studying modern banking, especially the central bank system, as the Japanese government had decided to establish one (Shizume 2020: 239–240). Matsutaka consulted Léon Say (1826–1896), the French finance minister, and Say advised him to study the Belgian system because it had been established recently (in 1850) and was well-documented as a law and easy to introduce from scratch.

Léon Say, the grandson of Jean-Baptiste Say (1767–1832), was a French economist who advocated economic liberalism and free trade, opposing socialism and government interventions. He served as finance minister in 1872–1873, 1875–1879, and 1882. During his first term as finance minister (1872–1873), he completed the payment of the massive Franco-Prussian War indemnity of five million franc (200 million pounds). During Matsukata's stay in Paris, Say presided over an international monetary conference in August 1878, one of a series of failed attempts to stabilize gold–silver parity (bimetallism) as proposed by the United States, triggered by the move to gold by the unified Germany. Later, Say led the move by member states of the Latin Monetary Union (France, Belgium, Italy, and Switzerland) to completely stop the minting of silver coins in October that year (Ericson 2019: 38–41).

In essence, Say taught Matsukata three things—how to establish a national central bank, the quantity theory of money, and the risk of foreign borrowing. With regard to the first, Say advised Matsukata to study the recently established Belgian National Bank, as mentioned above. Following the advice, the BOJ was modeled after the Belgian central banking system (Shizume 2018a). With regard to the second point, Say introduced Matsukata to *Traité de la scence des finances* by Pierre Paul Leroy-Beaulieu (1843–1916), which had been published just the previous year (Ericson 2019: 41–45). Matsukata learned from the book that "the domestic supply of banknotes would determine the value of the currency, measured by its price on the foreign exchange market" (Flandreau 2003: 16). This was precisely the point for which Matsukata criticized Ōkuma's easy monetary policy in 1880. With regard to the third point, Say's experience of war indemnity payments had taught Matsukata about the sins of foreign indebtedness. It was conceivable that Say might have shared his debt repayment experience with Matsutaka.[11]

Despite their stay in Paris coinciding, Maeda and Matsukata obtained different knowledge from different mentors. Maeda learned about development strategies, while Matsukata learned about public finance and monetary system stability.

References

Banno, Junji. 2014. *Japan's modern history, 1857–1937: a new political narrative*. Oxfordshire, England; New York: Routledge.

Bordo, Michael D., and Hugh Rockoff. 1996. The gold standard as a good housekeeping seal of approval. *Journal of Economic History* 56 (2): 389–428.

Court of Audit (France) website. Publication date unknown. TISSERAND Louis Eugène: www.ccomptes.fr/fr/biographies/tisserand-louis-eugene (Accessed on 19 Mar 2021).

Eichengreen, Barry. 1992. *Golden fetters: the gold standard and the Great Depression, 1919–1939*. New York: Oxford University Press.

Ericson, Steven J. 2019. *Financial stabilization in Meiji Japan: the impact of the Matsukata reform*. Cornell University Press.

Flandreau, Marc. 2003. Crises and punishment: moral hazard and the pre-1914 international financial architecture. Marc Flandreau ed. *Money doctors: the experience of international financial advising, 1850–2000*. London: Routledge: 13–48.

Fukai, Eigo. 1941. *Kaiko nanajūnen (Reflections on the past seventy years)*. Tokyo: Iwanami shoten.

Keynes, John Maynard, and Hubert Douglas Henderson. 1929. Can Lloyd George do it? An examination of the Liberal pledge. *The Nation and Athenaeum* May 1 1929. London: 2–44.

Metzler, Mark. 2006. *Lever of empire: The international gold standard and the crisis of liberalism in prewar Japan*. Berkeley and Los Angeles: University of California Press.

Nanto Dick K., and Shinji Takagi. 1985. Korekiyo Takahashi and Japan's recovery from the Great Depression. *American Economic Review* 75 (2): 369–374.

Shizume, Masato. 2009a. *Sekai kyōkō to keizai seisaku: kaihō shōkoku Nihon no keiken to gendai* (The world depression and economic policy: lessons from Japan as a small open economy). Tokyo: Nikkei Shinbun Shuppan Sha.

Shizume, Masato. 2009b. The Japanese economy during the interwar period: instability in the financial system and the impact of the world depression. *Bank of Japan Review* 2009-E-2.

Shizume, Masato. 2018a. A history of the Bank of Japan, 1882–2016. Jacobson, Tor, Daniel Waldenström, and Rodney Edvinsson eds. *Sveriges Riksbank 350 years: a central bank in a world of central banks*. Cambridge, UK: Cambridge University Press: 328–360.

Shizume, Masato. 2018b. Financial crises and the central bank: lessons from Japan during the 1920s. Rockoff, Hugh, and Isao Suto eds. *Coping with financial crises: some lessons from financial history*. Singapore: Springer Nature: 131–148.

Shizume, Masato. 2020. Nihon ni okeru kindai shin'yō kahei eno ikō (The transition towards a modern credit money in Japan). Shizume, Masato ed. *Shin'yō kahei no seisei to tenkai (The emergence and development of credit money)*. Tokyo: Keio University Press: 221–255.

Shizume, Masato. 2021. Kansenshō no rekishi kara nani o manabuka: Meiji-Taishō ki no Nihon no keiken o fumaete (What we learn from the history of pandemics? Lessons from Japan during the Meiji-Taishō Era). *Keizai Kenkyū* 72: 209–227.

[11] Ericson (2019: 40) also mentions Jean-Baptiste Krantz (1817–1899), a civil engineer and commissioner-general of Exposition Universelle, who emphasized the risk of foreign borrowing using the example of the French railroad loan from British investors.

Smethurst, Richard J. 2007. *From foot soldier to finance minister: Takahashi Korekiyo, Japan's Keynes*. Cambridge, MA: Harvard University Asia Center, 292.
Soda, Osamu. 2017. *Chihōsangyō no kindaika kōsō: Maeda Masana no shisō to kōdō* (A strategy for the modernization of regional industries: thoughts and actions of Maeda Masana). Tokyo: Nōrin Tōkei Kyōkai.
Takahashi, Korekiyo. 1936a. *Zuisōroku* (Memoir). Tokyo: Chikura Shobō.
Takahashi, Korekiyo. 1936b. *Keizairon* (Economics). Tokyo: Chikura Shobō.

Chapter 6
Lessons for Today from Takahashi Korekiyo's Policies

This chapter concludes with lessons for today, focusing on challenges Takahashi faced, policy innovations he and his colleague introduced, and broader implications for the domestic political economy and geopolitics in the Asia–Pacific region. From a pure economic perspective, the challenges he faced were comparable to those of policymakers in an emerging economy today. However, the biggest challenge for him was the crisis of fiscal policy governance, which also related to Japan's primary national goal.

6.1 Challenges Takahashi Faced

As Inoue (2012: 240–241) indicates, the party cabinet in the early 1930s faced a triple crisis on the economic, international relations, and domestic politics fronts, namely, the Great Depression, confrontation with China, and terrorism. The Japanese economy had been dealt a double blow by the return to the gold standard and the global depression. The Mukden Incident in September 1931 sparked tensions between Japan and China, and the Tokyo government was on the way to losing control of the Kwantung Army stationed in Manchuria. Terrorists had killed leaders from both political parties, former Finance Minister Inoue Junnosuke of the Minseitō in February 1932, and Prime Minister Inukai Tsuyoshi of the Seiyūkai in May 1932.

I have shown how Takahashi fought well on the economic front with his macroeconomic stimulus package comprising exchange rate, monetary, and fiscal policies, achieving an early recovery from the depression. From a purely macroeconomic policy perspective, Takahashi's policy package achieved great success. It brought the Japanese economy out of the Great Depression despite adverse external conditions.

From an economic perspective, the challenges Takahashi faced were comparable with those of policymakers in a small, open, emerging market economy during and

M. Shizume, *The Japanese Economy During the Great Depression*,
Studies in Economic History,
https://doi.org/10.1007/978-981-13-7357-2_6

after the 1990s. Facing the macroeconomic policy trilemma, he prescribed a one-shot devaluation of the national currency to emerge from the Great Depression as a "money doctor." His remedy is comparable to those taken by emerging market economies during the 1997–1998 financial crisis (Shizume 2009: 238–240). It is also consistent with the "fear of floating," a theory that holds that it is not very easy for policymakers in a small, open economy to follow the textbook solution of floating exchange rates, and that many countries take the option of introducing a managed float or a soft peg regime though officially calling it a floating regime (Calvo and Reinhart 2002).

Realizing that the core of the second and third problems were the governance of military operations, which tended to overreach, Takahashi proceeded further. Following the precedent of a top-down approach in the 1920s, which had worked well with the cooperation of Army Minister Tanaka Giichi, he tried to establish a new body for the civilian control of the military comprising the prime minister, the finance minister, the foreign minister, and two military ministers.

Had both the parties fully supported his effort, it might have worked. The two parties were given many opportunities to cooperate with each other to overcome the crises, and some members did make concessions. However, they failed to form a united government, attacked each other, and eventually lost public support. When the public expressed its concern over military aggression and ballooning government debt in the February 1936 general election, another terrorist attack took the life of Takahashi, the icon of fiscal discipline and the principal obstacle to military expansionism.

6.2 The 1930s from a Longer Perspective

Recent studies of modern Japanese history have revealed that there was no single turning point in the change from a cooperative policy to a unilateral one on the international front, or from a liberal democratic policy to a totalitarian one. Even so, the 1930s marked a decisive period in terms of Japan's economic and political history both from the external and domestic points of view.

The Meiji Government set a dual mandate of "rich country, strong military" for its modernization project. However, the tensions between the "rich country" and "strong military" goals of this dual mandate, which existed right from the onset of Japan's modernization, were the source of the biggest challenges faced by Takahashi and the Japanese government as a whole.

In the 1870s, within the oligarchical government, a faction of veterans of the previous civil war with the Tokugawa Shogunate sought to expand their power through gunboat diplomacy toward neighboring countries. Ōkubo Toshimichi, the then effective prime minister, rejected the veterans' idea because he recognized that Japan lacked the economic power to conduct such a military operation.

Tensions arose again at the turn of the century. By then, Japan had laid the foundations for a modern fiscal state and constitutional monarchy in which two competing political groups played a political game to further their own interests. The first group, which prioritized the goal of a "strong military," comprised veterans of past civil wars and emerging bureaucrats from the administrative branch. The other group was made up of civilian taxpayers largely comprising landowners, who had power in the House of Representatives (He 2013: 128–130; Banno 2014: 118–119). Also, Japan was on the verge of a transition from a defensive stance toward international relations, aimed at avoiding colonization, to a more aggressive one, aimed at building its own empire in Asia.

The government found a solution to its financing problems—namely, to borrow from abroad. It succeeded in massive fundraising during the Russo-Japanese War even though the burden of debt servicing cast a shadow over the future of its public finances. At that time, the government carefully calculated the stakes and considered the risk of pursuing one of the two goals, a "strong military," at the expense of the other goal, a "rich country," and the army and the navy followed the government's policies as a whole.

World War I and the subsequent international disarmament eased tensions at least temporarily; on the one hand, Japan, removed from the main battlefield in Europe, achieved robust economic growth and expanded its economic capacity during the war, even though the Japanese economy suffered deflation and financial instability after the war. On the other hand, postwar international disarmament restricted military competition between the major powers, bringing peace dividends including for Japan, while the empire-building effort continued. Industrialization and urbanization associated with economic growth resulted in the emergence of new classes of people such as business elites and factory workers in urban areas. In domestic politics, universal male suffrage was established in 1925, and a two-party system comprising the conservative Seiyūkai and the liberal Kenseikai-Minseitō emerged in the House of Representatives. The two-party system was expected to coordinate various interests and reconcile the conflict between the "strong military" and "rich country" goals of the government's dual mandate.

Tensions heightened during the late 1920s and the early 1930s. The Kwantung Army, which was stationed in Manchuria to defend the lives and properties of Japanese citizens, tried to expand its sphere to include the whole of Manchuria and beyond without the consent of the Tokyo government. The party governments had managed to control it until the outbreak of the Mukden Incident in September 1931. Subsequently, however, it lost control by endorsing the army's preemptive actions and allowing it to conduct military operations before obtaining the consent of the Tokyo government. Some later observers suggest that the party governments could have succeeded in civilian control of the army had both parties cooperated with each other to defend democracy (Inoue 2012; Banno 2014). However, they fought between themselves and attacked one another. Some politicians in the Seiyūkai even appeased the army to get its support. In this sense, the army's aggressiveness was further encouraged by the political parties' incapability to deal with it, thereby paving the way for a devastating simultaneous all-out war with China and the United States.

Japan deviated from its long-standing policy of cooperation with its Anglo-American allies in the 1930s. From the first visit of Commodore Perry in 1853 and the opening of the treaty ports in 1859, Japan had based its international relations on cooperation with the major powers, especially the United States and Great Britain. The United States had been Japan's biggest trading partner despite some conflicts of interest in China. The United States imported silk and other goods from Japan, while Japan depended on resources and technologies from the United States. Great Britain was a major strategic partner—Japan had shared interests with Great Britain on the east Asian continent and depended on its technologies and financial markets. However, two events in September 1931, the Mukden Incident and Britain's departure from the gold standard, undermined the basic conditions for the previous cooperative policies.

Takahashi's stance was to preserve cooperation with Japan's traditional allies, the United States and Great Britain, while alleviating the negative impact from these incidents on the domestic economy. Even though Takahashi imposed a gold embargo in December 1931, he resisted eliminating the yen's link with gold, presumably expecting to eventually return to gold at a new parity reflecting the fundamentals of the Japanese economy, when the gold standard would be finally restored. Takahashi also made efforts to avoid excessive military spending and to control overseas military operations. While his main motivation might have been concern for fiscal sustainability, his policies were also consistent with the international cooperation policies of his predecessor Inoue from the Minseitō.

Takahashi's efforts were cut short by his assassination, but the parliamentary system continued to exist, elections continued to be held, though with political repression, and cabinets were formed under the constitution. However, the parliament exhausted its political capital following the assassination of Takahashi and his colleagues (Inoue 2012: 193–235). After the Second Sino-Japanese War broke out in 1937, the two parties decided to cooperate, and merged into the Imperial Rule Assistance Association (Taisei-yokusan-kai) in 1940 to support mobilization toward war. The parliament kept approving skyrocketing military budgets towards the end of World War II, while a small number of politicians from the original two parties, as well as some other opposition parties, survived politically through the war.

Ishibashi Tanzan's journal *Tōyō Keizai Shinpō*, which supported Takahashi's currency depreciation, easy money, and fiscal stimulus, and advocated a reduction in military spending, also survived. Upon the unconditional surrender of Japan to the Allies in August 1945, Ishibashi declared that, freed from military constraints, Japan would revive and benefit from tremendous opportunities for utilizing its human capital for civilian purposes (Ishibashi 1945). For Ishibashi, this was the return to normalcy. In 1946, Ishibashi was appointed finance minister in the Yoshida Shigeru Cabinet, led by a former diplomat who pursued lightly armed forces to pave the way for rapid postwar growth. Therefore, in a sense, Takahashi's goal was finally achieved after World War II (Column of this chapter: 6.5 Takahashi Korekiyo and Ishibashi Tanzan).

6.3 Lessons for Today

6.3.1 *Macroeconomic Policy Innovations and the Unconventional Policy*

Today, central banks in mature economies—such as Japan, the United States, and Europe—faced with zero lower bound (ZLB) are pursuing unconventional monetary policy, the exit from which seems a long way away, and as yet undiscovered by these central banks. Can Takahashi's experiences have any lessons for us in this regard? Though the situation Takahashi faced was distinct from those faced by policymakers in mature economies in the twenty-first century, we may still learn lessons from his experiences.

First, we may learn from Takahashi's ideas regarding the effect of macroeconomic policy on the supply side of the economy. While conventional arguments today focus on the effects of monetary policy on the demand side of the economy, the BOJ's low interest rate policy together with Japan's financial sector supported the rapid post-World War II economic growth of Japan from both demand and supply sides (Shizume 2018). Metzler (2013) relates the high growth of the Japanese economy to Schumpeterian ideas of finance-led economic development. While Takahashi did not mention Schumpeter, he emphasized the role of the financial sector as an incubator of innovation and a source of economic development (Chap. 5 of this volume). In a sense, he laid the groundwork for the post-World War II high growth regime represented by Prime Minister Ikeda Hayato's Income-Doubling Plan of 1960.[1] Takahashi's economic ideas and their origins, as well as the policy tools he employed, are interesting topics for exploring macroeconomic policy goals and instruments.

Second, Takahashi's experience shows us how difficult it is to exit an unconventional policy. Shima (1983: 120) argues that the scheme of government bond underwriting by the BOJ lacked an exit policy. According to Shima, on the one hand, if expectations of interest rate hikes had arisen in the markets, investors would have held back to make gradual tightening of monetary policy impossible. On the other hand, if the central bank had attempted a swift tightening, it would have caused a collapse in the prices of government bonds. In the end, the BOJ would not have been able to tighten monetary policy either gradually or swiftly due to its scheme of underwriting government bonds.

As I showed in previous chapters, the monetary policy scheme implemented by Team Takahashi itself lacked an exit mechanism from such an unconventional situation. However, triggered by a signal in the financial markets indicating the approaching limit of market capacity, Team Takahashi tried to correct the policy course manually by negotiating budget cuts including cuts in military spending. In doing so, Takahashi tried to build a complementary scheme at the ministerial level,

[1] Ikeda joined the MOF in 1925 and once resigned due to illness in 1931, before Takahashi's return to office, and returned to the MOF in 1934. Despite never working with Takahashi, Ikeda had the chance to read Takahashi's writings, see the consequences of his policies, and to learn from them.

recognizing the limited capacity of the parliament at that time. His attempt was rejected by the army minister and ended with the tragedy of his assassination in a terrorist attack.

The scheme of open market operations introduced by Takahashi was maintained until the end of World War II in 1945, with the BOJ extending liquidity provision in the financial markets to accommodate fiscal expenditure. In a sense, monetary policy supported the government's intent of war right up to the last minute, and rampant inflationary pressures during and after the war was the price paid.

In short, the lesson for today from Takahashi's attempt at an exit policy is that, unless the original cause of disequilibrium is removed, exit from the unconventional policy may not be possible. In the early 1930s, Team Takahashi made monetary policy innovations to accommodate fiscal demand and, thereby, avoid turbulences in the financial market. Takahashi realized that the core of the problem was fiscal policy governance—an old policy issue that persisted, even though the source of the problem varied at different times.

6.3.2 Civilian Control of Military Forces

In parliamentary democracies, the annual budget in general needs to be approved by the parliament before it can be implemented. Under authoritarian rule, it is conceivable that such a governance mechanism does not work. But even in a parliamentary democracy, the governance of fiscal policy remains debatable. Takahashi's attempt and its eventual failure provide an illuminating example of the collapse of budgetary management within a system of parliamentary democracy.

As I showed in Chap. 5 of this volume, a version of parliamentary democracy emerged in Japan in the 1920s. Recent studies on modern Japanese political history reveal that the Meiji Constitution regime was not an authoritarian system by nature, but had a carefully designed system of checks and balances for budgetary management. During the Russo-Japanese War and after World War I, the Japanese polity showed considerable resilience against challenges to the sustainability of public finance both in war and peace times.

The two-party system, with the Seiyūkai and the Kenseikai-Minseitō, was expected to serve as a check to the administrative branch. The process by which the central government lost control of overseas military operations in the Mukden Incident shows us the crucial role of communication within the administrative branch. The internal battles between the two parties in the parliament interfered with the formation of an effective counterbalance against the extremists in the military and the appeasement of the military by the legislative branch.

Simply institutionalizing a system, such as a parliamentary democracy or of checks and balances for national budget management, does not guarantee that the system will work. It is human agency that operates and makes the system work. In this volume, to highlight this point, I have traced both Takahashi's intention to make the system work and the consequences of his efforts. When he returned to the office of the finance minister in 1931, Takahashi was with Prime Minister Inukai Tsuyoshi, with Tanaka Giichi having passed away in 1929. Inoue Junnosuke, while in the opposition party, was still alive and would become the opposition leader. These people were his political capital in his attempts at achieving cooperation between the two parties. However, both Inoue and Inukai were assassinated in 1932, and no one could replace them.

The list of postwar prime ministers and most of their stances toward civilian control of the military forces reveals the legacy of Takahashi, who fought for it. Three of Japan's post-World War II prime ministers had seats in the House of Representatives during Takahashi's term in the 1930s: Ashida Hitoshi (prime minister: March–October 1948) and Hatoyama Ichirō (1954–1956) belonged to the Seiyūkai, and Katayama Tetsu (1947–1948) belonged to the Shakai Taishūtō (the Social Mass Party). Yoshida Shigeru (1946–1947, 1948–1954) had been a diplomat, Kishi Nobusuke (1957–1960), Ikeda Hayato (1960–1964), Satō Eisaku (1964–1972), and Fukuda Takeo (1976–1978) bureaucrats, and Ishibashi Tanzan (1956–1957) a journalist during Takahashi's term. All of them witnessed Takahashi's activities in the government and the abrupt end to them. Miki Takeo (1974–1976) and Ōhira Masayoshi (1978–1980) were college students during Takahashi's term in the 1930s; Miki joined the House of Representatives in 1937 as a non-partisan politician with the aim of defending democracy, while Ōhira became a bureaucrat in 1936 through the recommendation of Tsushima Juichi, one of Takahashi's subordinates in the MOF.[2]

Bohn (1998, 2008) argue that the US political system has made national debt sustainable through history. Bohn (2008) looks at US public debt from 1791 to 2003, and concludes that the government has continued to respond to higher debt-to-GDP ratios with contractionary fiscal policies. A comparative study of different governments may be a topic for future research.

In short, though Takahashi's assassination temporarily marked the loss of civilian control, later politicians learned their lesson from his efforts and the subsequent deviation from the principle of civilian control of the military.

6.3.3 Geopolitics and the National Goal

What was the alternative then? This is a question about the national goal beyond macroeconomic policy. One possibility would have been to contain military aggression against China, instead concentrating on economic interests on the continent. In fact, in the 1920s, Takahashi and Ishibashi echoed each other on cooperation with Japan's big and old neighbor, China. As Dickinson (2007: 210) asserts, referring to earlier studies, Japan's presence in China until the formal outbreak of war in 1937

[2] In 1945, Kishi was arrested on charges of war crimes by the GHQ/SCAP. In 1946, Hatoyama and Ishibashi were purged from public service even though the charge against them, especially for Ishibashi, was debatable.

was primarily a commercial venture, and Japanese wartime planning for the Second Sino-Japanese and Pacific Wars were contingent in nature.

Mosk (2007: 207) summarizes the military strategy of Japan from the 1890s to the mid-1930s as "taking on one enemy at a time, forming alliances with third parties in order to keep Japan's military out of wars that pitted it against massive alliances." Takahashi's era in the early 1930s marked a transition from the above strategy to "an overreaching military strategy, fighting throughout the Eurasian landmass while simultaneously taking on the two great Anglo-American maritime powers on the waters of the Pacific."

In the end, Japan chose military aggression in Asia and the Pacific in the late 1930s and the early 1940s. In a sense, Japan prioritized a "strong military" over a "rich country" as its national goal, deviating from the principle of balancing the two goals.

The price of the choice was enormous: lacking the material basis for sustainability, the Japanese empire's strategy for wartime economy, the Great East Asia Co-prosperity Sphere, proved to be pie in the sky. Eventually, Japan lost all of its overseas territories, over two million lives including both soldiers and civilians, and the trust of its neighbors. Many of its cities were destroyed by air raids, including the two atomic bombs on Hiroshima and Nagasaki. On the Chinese mainland, the Nationalist Party, Japan's main enemy on the mainland during World War II, and the Communist Party fought each other after the defeat of their common enemy, Japan. The Communists ousted the Nationalists to Taiwan and declared the establishment of the People's Republic of China in 1949. After this, China virtually disappeared as a potential market from the sights of the Japanese business community for three decades until it opened its doors to the capitalist world again.

As Ishibashi correctly stated, Japan's defeat gave it a chance to understand the intentions of Takahashi and Ishibashi in the 1920s. The preamble to the new Constitution of Japan of 1946 stipulates: "We, the Japanese people, desire peace for all time and are deeply conscious of the high ideals controlling human relationship, and we have determined to preserve our security and existence, trusting in the justice and faith of the peace-loving peoples of the world." Article 9 of the Constitution stipulates:

> Aspiring sincerely to an international peace based on justice and order, the Japanese people forever renounce war as a sovereign right of the nation and the threat or use of force as means of settling international disputes.
>
> In order to accomplish the aim of the preceding paragraph, land, sea, and air forces, as well as other war potential, will never be maintained. The right of belligerency of the state will not be recognized.[3]

The preamble and the first paragraph of Article 9 rephrase the Kellogg–Briand Pact of 1928, which outlawed war, and Japan ratified this. The second paragraph went beyond the pact by dismissing the maintenance of military forces. While these clauses were drafted by GHQ/SCAP, the Japanese people accepted them after Japan

[3] The Constitution of Japan, from the National Diet Library website: www.ndl.go.jp/constitution/e/etc/c01.html. (accessed on March 7, 2021).

gained independence by the San Francisco Treaty in 1951 and have preserved them to date. Prime Minister Yoshida Shigeru pursued the so-called "Yoshida doctrine" prioritizing a "rich country" over a "strong military." While Japan established the National Police Reserve (now the Self-Defense Forces) upon the outbreak of the Korean War in 1950, the Japanese government has kept its military presence to a bare minimum. Though some observers argue that the new constitution was forced on Japan by the GHQ/SCAP, historians suggest that the Japanese people voluntarily accepted the constitution as the basic principle underlying the postwar national goal (Nakamura 2012: 520; Takeda 2008: 71). The high economic growth of the post-war Japanese economy proved the rationale of Takahashi and Ishibashi's claim.

In short, without the military domination of East Asia, Japan achieved remarkable economic development and finally caught up to the Western powers in around the early 1970s, achieving its long-standing national goal since the opening of the treaty ports in the mid-nineteenth century.

6.4 Conclusion

Today, in the early 2020s, 90 years since Takahashi's return to office in 1931, the world faces multiple challenges. On the economic front, the debate around secular stagnation has entered a new phase with the spread of COVID-19, and the enormous supply and demand shocks that resulted in negative global economic growth for the first time since the Great Depression in the 1930s. On the political front, parliamentary democracies are facing serious challenges in many countries, not only in emerging market economies but also in the developed world, including the United States. On the global geopolitical front, China is emerging as a global power and is seen to be a new challenger to US dominance since the breakdown of the Soviet Union and the former Communist bloc.

To conclude this volume, I will summarize the lessons learned from Japan's experience in the 1930s, which can be applied to aspects of the economy, national politics, and global geopolitics today.

First, Takahashi's innovative macroeconomic policy package provided an effective remedy for demand-led depression and deflation. As a "money doctor," his cure—a combination of currency depreciation, fiscal stimulus, and easy money—had an immediate effect on the national economy, bringing robust growth along with mild inflation. From a purely economic perspective, his team had the expertise required to manage the national economy and the financial markets. They provide a superb example for policymakers in small, open economies. The choice made in terms of the exchange rate level had a crucial effect on kickstarting economic recovery, while the accommodative monetary policy had an enduring effect in terms of supporting the recovery. Though fiscal policy had a limited effect in this case, that was due to its contents: the effect of military expenses for overseas operations may have eroded and weakened the expenditure multiplier effect. On the practical side, Team Takahashi made innovations in the market operation of monetary policy, which was also used to manage the wartime economy.

Second, on the domestic political front, the biggest challenge for an exit from Takahashi's unconventional policy lay in the political economics of fiscal policy governance. In this period in Japan, the single most significant expansionary pressure on the national budget came from military expenditure toward empire building. The existing checks-and-balances system of a parliamentary democracy did not work, and the right-wing faction and extremists in the military used physical power in the form of terrorism and coup attempts to remove obstacles from their path.

On this front, Japan's experience in the 1930s is not far removed from the present day, as recent developments in the emerging world demonstrate the vulnerability of democracy. Japan's failure in the 1930s is a negative example we can learn from.

At the same time, the survivors of a collapsed democracy went on to serve as leaders in postwar Japan. The Japanese people, and the country as a whole, having once failed to maintain democratic control of the national budget and to define a practical national goal, learned their lessons from the collapse of democracy. Japan's postwar democracy was not an institution imported from the West. It was built on the foundation of previous experience and the political capital of domestic politicians and electorates.

Third, in the geopolitics of the modern Asia–Pacific region, the emergence of Japan as a new aggressive power brought tremendous tensions with other powers in the region, especially with China and the United States. Though the constellation has changed, Japan's failure to build a cooperative system in the region may offer some lessons for the emerging powers of the twenty-first century. Japan's post-World War II strategy of a "wealthy nation without a strong military" brought overall benefits for the Asia–Pacific region that the pre-World War II strategy of "wealthy nation, strong military" could not bring. The lesson here is not just for Japan, but also for other emerging powers including China and other future powers with potential.

6.5 Column: Takahashi Korekiyo and Ishibashi Tanzan

Ishibashi Tanzan (1884–1973) was born in Tokyo to a Buddhist monk. After graduating from the Department of Philosophy, Waseda University, he joined the *Tōyō Keizai Shinpō*, one of Japan's leading economic journals, in 1911, and soon became the chief editor. He continued to serve as an economic journalist and was a fair critic of the government, businesses, and financial institutions until 1946, when he gave up journalism to become the finance minister in the Yoshida Cabinet. Despite never traveling abroad, he kept up with contemporary economics and the world economy by reading books, journal articles, and newspapers both in English and Japanese. He also regularly published articles on Japanese economic and policy issues, at first only in Japanese and then both in Japanese and English from 1934 onward. The first 15 years of his career as an economic journalist overlapped with Takahashi's career as a policymaker in his roles as governor of the BOJ and finance minister.

Ishibashi's editorials had a global and long-term perspective. In 1916, he predicted that the core of economic development in the twentieth century would be based on human resources and an improvement in the quality of life rather than on a mere increase in material quantity. He also argued that expenditure toward education, health, and improvements in the social environment was "productive," in the sense that it would increase human capital or improve the quality of life, while military expenditure was "not productive," because it did not contribute either to an increase in human capital or an improvement in the quality of life (Ishibashi 1916).

In 1921, Ishibashi published a series of editorials on the Washington Naval Disarmament Conference. He criticized the Japanese government's military expansionism and urged the government to abandon all overseas interest in East Asia, thereby leading international cooperation ahead of the Western powers. He estimated the costs and benefits of maintaining overseas territories, compared it against the net benefit from international trade gains without having to maintain territories, and concluded that the net benefit from international trade minus territories would exceed the net benefit from maintaining territories (Ishibashi 1921a).

Ishibashi further went on to publish a set of proposals in English aimed at the international community. The proposals included a total elimination of imperialistic demands, which could be the seeds of international disputes, the removal of protections and full adoption of free trade on a global scale, the establishment of self-determination and the total elimination of intervention of any kind in the Asia–Pacific region, the total abolition of the army, and the limiting of the navy to coast guards (Ishibashi 1921b).

From around 1924 onward, Ishibashi and his colleagues at the *Tōyō Keizai Shinpō* engaged in a policy campaign to return to the gold standard at a devalued parity of the yen. Ishibashi argued that that would be the best way to resume gold convertibility with minimal cost for the Japanese economy. He harshly criticized the Hamaguchi Cabinet's austerity policy, as Takahashi did (Ishibashi 1929). Ishibashi during this period, however, fell back on Gustav Cassel's theory of purchasing power parity rather than on Keynes' theory. He later said, "in the late 1920s and the early 1930s, Keynes was not so popular in Japan."

When the outline of Takahashi's stimulus package appeared in the summer of 1932, Ishibashi expressed full support for Takahashi's policy. In April 1935, ten months before Takahashi's assassination, he interviewed Takahasahi, and this became the only record of a direct conversation between the two men during Takahashi's term in the early 1930s. They agreed that the main goal of economic policy was to achieve full employment and on the positive effects of low interest rates and an easy money policy. When Ishibashi questioned Takahashi about the effects of military spending, Takahashi responded that some military expenditures could be productive. Ishibashi wrote a supplementary article in June, stating that "Mr Takahashi's intent was to say that military expenses could have a demand effect that could help reach full employment. If all workers made only weapons and gunboats, the nation cannot produce food, clothes, houses, or even the machinery required to manufacture weapons and gunboats. When the stocks of such items are exhausted, the national product would perish" (Ishibashi 1935a, b). Given that Takahashi and Ishibashi shared the same view on the risk of military spending, and that the interview was held less than a year before Takahashi's assassination, Ishibashi may have spoken for the finance minister, who was in a vulnerable position that did not allow him to openly criticize the military.

Ishibashi's argument was similar to Takahashi's in fundamental ways—the goal of full employment, an opposition to austerity in order to maintain an artificial exchange rate, and an awareness of the risk of military expansionism (Kyō 1992: 382–400). Both Ishibashi and Takahashi evaluated policies based on data and other empirical evidence. Both had global and long-term perspectives. And, needless to say, both employed macroeconomic elements even before the publication of Keynes' *General Theory*. Ishibashi and Takahashi both referred to Adam Smith, Alfred Marshall, and Friedrich List. Both were known to have read Karl Marx and, while neither used the logic of class struggle, they were both inclined toward Sidney Webb's Fabian socialism.

Ishibashi and the *Tōyō Keizai Shinpō* survived through World War II. In 1934, Ishibashi began publishing *The Oriental Economist*, a journal in English, which, surprisingly, continued being published throughout the war years (Ikeo 2020). Ishibashi had opposed the Great East Asia Co-Prosperity Sphere as an obstacle to free trade and its benefits and criticized the excessive burden of military spending in defense of the people's lives. He had been under surveillance as an anti-nationalistic liberal figure during the war (Ishibashi 1951: 271–272). The day after the emperor announced Japan's surrender in a radio address (August 15, 1945), Ishibashi wrote an article titled "The launch of a new Japan: a promising future," stating that no artificial restraints can impede the activities of the human brain and its products, and urged people to carry on with the spirit of science in a broader sense, not merely restraining themselves to material pursuit (Ishibashi 1945).

Ishibashi served as finance minister (1946–1947) in the Yoshida Cabinet. He opposed by the General Headquarters of the Supreme Commander for the Allied Powers' (GHQ/SCAP) policy of restraint to curb inflation, insisting that the true problem was not inflation, but the bottleneck in the supply of essential materials such as coal and steel. Presumably because of this, he was purged on a charge of war crimes, which he did not appear to be guilty of (Takemae 2002; Ikeo 2018).

In his career as an economics journalist and a policymaker, Ishibashi proved himself a close colleague and successor of Takahashi.

References

Banno, Junji. 2014. *Japan's modern history, 1857–1937: a new political narrative*. Oxfordshire, England; New York: Routledge.

Bohn, Henning. 1998. The behavior of U.S. public debt and deficits. *Quarterly Journal of Economics* 113(3): 949–963.

Bohn, Henning. 2008. The sustainability of fiscal policy in the United States. Neck, Reinhard, and Jan-Egbert Sturm eds. *Sustainability of public debt*. Cambridge, MA: MIT Press: 15–49.

Calvo, Guillermo. A., and Carmen. M. Reinhart. 2002. Fear of floating. *Quarterly Journal of Economics* 117: 379–408.
Dickinson, Frederick R. 2007. External relations. Tsutsui, William M. ed. *A companion to Japanese history*. Malden, MA: Blackwell Publishing Ltd: 207–223.
He, Wenkai. 2013. *Paths toward the modern fiscal state: England, Japan, and China*. Cambridge, MA: Harvard University Press.
Ikeo, Aiko. 2020. Tanzan Ishibashi's wartime journalistic activities and offering of information to overseas. *Ishibashi Tanzan Studies* 3: 121–148.
Ikeo, Aiko. 2018. American economists on Ishibashi Tanzan: Tracing the debate over the post-war inflation. *History of Japanese Economic Thought* 18: 1–19.
Inoue, Toshikazu. 2012. *Seiyūkai to minseitō* (The Seiyūkai and the Minseitō). Tokyo: Chūkō Shinsho.
Ishibashi, Tanzan. 1916. Kitarubeki hito chūshin no sangyō kakumei (Coming industrial revolution centered on humanity). *Tōyō Keizai Shinpō* September 5 1916.
Ishibashi, Tanzan. 1921a. Issai o sutsuru no kakugo: Taiheiyō kaigi ni taisuru waga taido (The preparation to abandon everything: the attitude toward the Pacific Conference). *Tōyō Keizai Shinpō* July 23 1921.
Ishibashi, Tanzan. 1921b. Gunbi seigen narabini taiheiyō oyobi kyokutō mondai ni kansuru kaigi ni tsuiteno kankoku (A recommendation to the conference for disarmament and East Asia-Pacific issues). *Tōyō Keizai Shinpō* September 24 1921.
Ishibashi, Tanzan. 1929. *Kin-kaikin no eikyōto taisaku: shin-heika kin-kaikin no teishō* (Effects of the lifting of gold embargo: a proposal for the lifting of gold embargo with a new parity). Tōyō Keizai Shinpōsha.
Ishibashi, Tanzan. 1935a. Takahashi Zōshō jūdan (An interview to Finance Minister Takahashi). *Tōyō Keizai Shinpō* May 4 1935.
Ishibashi, Tanzan. 1935b. Zaisei bōchō no jōgen to shūshuku no kagen: Takahashi zōshō no saikin no shinkyō o shindan su (The upper limit of fiscal expansion and the lower limit of contraction: evaluation of Finance Minister Takahashi's mind). *Tōyō Keizai Shinpō* June 15 1935.
Ishibashi, Tanzan. 1945. Kōsei Nihon no kadode: Zento wa jitsuni yōyō tari (A launch of new-born Japan: the promising future). *Tōyō Keizai Shinpō* August 25 1945.
Ishibashi, Tanzan. 1951. *Tanzan kaisō* (Reflections by Tanzan). Tokyo: Mainichi Shinbun Sha.
Kyō, Kokujitsu. 1992. *Ishibashi Tanzan no Shisō shi teki kenkyū* (A thesis on historical aspects of Ishibashi Tanzan's thoughts). Waseda University Press.
Metzler, Mark. 2013. *Capital as will and imagination: Schumpeter's guide to the postwar Japanese miracle*. Ithaca, NY: Cornell University Press.
Mosk, Carl. 2007. *Japanese economic development: Markets, norms, structures*. London: Routledge.
Nakamura, Takafusa. 2012. *Shōwa shi* (A history of the Shōwa period) 2. Tōyō Keizai Shinpōsha.
Shima, Kinzō. 1983. Iwayuru Takahashi zaisei ni tsuite (On so-called Takahashi economic policy). *Kin'yū Kenkyū* 2 (2), 83–124.
Shizume, Masato. 2009. *Sekai kyōkō to Keizai seisaku: kaihō shōkoku Nihon no keiken to gendai* (The world depression and economic policy: lessons from Japan as a small open economy). Tokyo: Nikkei Shinbun Shuppan Sha.
Shizume, Masato. 2018. Ishibashi Tanzan no keizaisisō no senkensei (Far-sightedness of Ishibashi Tanzan's economic thought). *Gakusai* 5: 72–85.
Takeda, Haruhito. 2008. *Kōdo Seichō* (The high growth). Iwanami Shoten.
Takemae, Eiji. 2002. *Inside GHQ: The allied occupation of Japan and its legacy*. Translated and adapted from the Japanese by Robert Ricketts and Sebastian Swann. New York: Continuum.

The manufacturer's authorised representative in the EU is Springer
Nature Customer Service Centre GmbH, Europaplatz 3, 69115 Heidelberg,
Germany. If you have any concerns regarding our products, please
contact ProductSafety@springernature.com

Printed and bound by CPI Group (UK) Ltd, Croydon, CR0 4YY
25/09/2026
02222892-0017